John Shepherd

SPORTS
TRAINING

THE COMPLETE GUIDE TO

A & C Black • London

First published 2006 by
A&C Black Publishers Ltd
38 Soho Square, London W1D 3HB
www.acblack.com

ISBN-10 0 713678356
ISBN-13 9780713678352

A CIP catalogue record for this book is available from the British Library.

Typeset in Baskerville by Palimpsest Book Production Ltd, Grangemouth, Stirlingshire

Cover image © Corbis
Inside photography by Grant Pritchard except image on page 184 © Corbis

A&C Black uses paper produced with elemental chlorine-free pulp, harvested from managed sustainable forests.

Printed and bound in Singapore

CONTENTS

This book is dedicated to my wife.

ACKNOWLEDGEMENTS

I would like to thank Robert Foss and Alex Hazle at A&C Black for supporting this project and Grant Pritchard for the great photography. Thanks also to Brunel University (my old stamping ground) for the use of their excellent facilities (it's a far cry from when I ran round a horseshoe shaped cinder running track as an undergraduate) and to Jo Christie, who modelled for the photographs.

INTRODUCTION

Recently, there has been an explosion in the availability of sports science; the web has obviously been highly instrumental in this. Unfortunately, as anyone who has read a 'learned' physical education/sports science journal, review or text will know, there's often a great deal of jargon and concepts can be difficult to understand. Coach and athlete want to know how to apply this knowledge quickly and practically; what training will make them quicker, stronger, more powerful, more agile, more enduring and so on? In writing this book I set out to do just that. I wanted to unravel the 'sports science mysteries' and provide athlete and coach with a practical understanding of sports science and training theory, so that they can produce personal bests and winning performances.

Sports training is all about making the right conditioning (training) choices for a particular sport and marrying them to the specific needs of the athlete and/or team. Believe it or not, in most cases the recipients cannot fail to win (or at least optimise their performance) when this 'marriage' is achieved.

The Complete Guide to Sports Training takes you from understanding the basic structure, movement and energy creation possibilities of the body, through to specific 'developmental' parts, such as, Developing Power, Developing Endurance and Developing Speed and Agility. These parts explain and, crucially, exemplify how the body can be optimally conditioned to achieve specific sports performance goals. Supporting parts consider nutrition and supplementation, coaching and mental training.

As an international athlete, sports science graduate, coach to international athletes and longtime sports, fitness and health writer, I have been fortunate to come into contact with, train with, work with and interview some of the most knowledgeable 'brains' in sport. I have assimilated as much of this knowledge as possible into this book; and to reiterate, I have tried to make it as accessible and practical as possible. To achieve this you'll find sample training programmes, sports training tips, boxes, panels and numerous photographs throughout, all designed to make the learning process simpler.

I have also included comment from top athletes and coaches, ranging from Olympic champions Seb Coe, Jason Gardener and Cathy Freeman to Rugby World Cup winner Josh Lewsey, all of whom I have been fortunate enough to interview and on occasions train with. After all, there is no more justification for a sports training ingredient, or 'way of doing', than seeing it manifest itself in elite-level winning performances. Read on, and you too could be achieving your very own world-beating and personal best-beating performance, or engendering one in those you coach.

John Shepherd

PART **ONE**

THE SPORTS MACHINE – THE HUMAN BODY

As an athlete in my younger days I was often told to do 'such and such' a workout with no rationale really being offered as to why it would benefit me. No mention, for example, was made of the muscular action involved, or even the specific muscles used in an exercise. Energy pathways meant little, if nothing, to me. As a result, I believe it is crucial for coach and athlete to understand the effect a particular workout has on the body. Knowing this will make the purpose of the workout clear and all the more likely to succeed. In this part I provide information on how the body works and, crucially, how it adapts to sports training. I explain the concepts behind much of the practical training information provided later in the book.

Please note that I use the word 'athlete' to refer to all sports performers.

Conditioning

Conditioning is the term used in the sports coaching/training world to refer to the process of improving the components of sports readiness, such as strength, speed, skill, agility, endurance and mental preparation.

Adaptation

Adaptation is the term given to the positive phys- iological changes that improve sports readiness. It should be noted that adaptation occurs when the body is resting, *not* when it is being trained.

The Body as 'Sports Machine'

The human body is, as often stated, a truly incredible machine. Carrying out our daily tasks involves a complicated synergy between mental, mechanical, chemical and electrical processes. It is in the sporting context that you realise just what the body is capable of as a 'sports machine', such as when you see an athlete like Carl Lewis running at close to 30mph and clearing nearly 9m in the long jump. However, even an athlete of Lewis's stature could not have reached his gold medal-winning potential had he not been supremely conditioned.

Specificity

Specificity of training is the key to optimum sports conditioning, whether the coach/athlete be after greater speed, endurance, strength or power.

Throughout the book I will return to this almost mantra-like requirement for successful sports condi- tioning. Athletes who do not heed this advice will not achieve their optimum potential.

Athlete Profile

Josh Lewsey, England rugby world cup winner, on the value of specificity

'Our whole fitness programme is based on trying to make it as game-related as possible. In the last five years there has been a big shift towards much more specific training. Ten years ago, rugby players used to go for 10-mile runs, but this is an ineffectual way of training. It gets rid of your fast twitch (speed and power) muscle fibres. What you need to do in rugby is sustain energy for 80 minutes, but this is in the form of lots of maximal bursts with very short recovery.'

In short, Lewsey describes rugby as a 'power endurance' sport (see page 169 for further infor- mation on training rugby players, and pages 166–69 for optimising team/field sports preparation). Fast twitch and slow twitch muscle fibres are covered in this part (see pages 10–13).

The Cardiovascular System

The cardiovascular system performs four vital functions under exercise conditions:

1 It pumps oxygenated blood around the body.
2 It returns blood to the lungs for aeration.
3 It transports heat from the body's core to the surface.
4 It delivers fuel nutrients to muscles and other active tissue.

The Heart

The heart is a muscle. It responds to (endurance) training in much the same way as skeletal muscle, such as the biceps, by increasing in size and strength/power.

The two major physiological responses of the heart to training are:

1 An increase in stroke volume
2 A decrease in heart rate

Stroke volume refers to the amount of blood that the heart can pump around the body. Elite endurance athletes can pump 35–40 litres of blood per minute, compared to the 20–22 litres achieved by healthy but untrained college-aged males. Females' stroke volumes will be around 25 per cent lower than males' as a consequence of their smaller stature.

Heart rate simply reflects the number of times that the heart beats. Heart rate is measured over a minute in beats per minute (bpm). It will decrease as a result of regular endurance training at sub-maximal exercise intensities (maximum heart rate – HRMax – will remain largely genetically determined). Coupled to increased stroke volume, this means that less effort is required to pump greater amounts of oxygenated blood around the body (oxygen, as will be noted later, is the key ingredient in generating aerobic energy).

Elite endurance athletes can have heart rates of 50 bpm (or less). This compares with the 75 bpm average for the healthy sedentary individual.

Arteries

Arteries transport oxygen-rich blood to the exercising muscles. Oxygenated blood passes through the main artery (the aorta), through smaller arteries (arterioles), to even smaller blood vessels (met-arterioles and capillaries) and into muscle tissue.

Training Improves the Oxygen Transport System

It is not just the heart that responds to endurance training; so too does the oxygen transport system. For example, in response to endurance training, more capillarisation will occur in muscles – with more capillaries, greater quantities of oxygenated blood and nutrients will reach muscles, increasing their ability to produce mostly aerobic energy.

Altitude Training and Red Blood Cell Count

There is around 20ml of oxygen in 100ml of blood. Altitude training methods (see page 124) attempt to increase red blood cell count and, consequently, the amount of oxygen arriving at the working muscles. As will be noted, there is considerable debate as to whether altitude training actually works.

Understanding the Energy-creation Processes

It is useful for coach and athlete to appreciate how energy is created (and replenished) in the body. This will enable them to understand how the different energy pathways work together to create energy, and how relevant physiological adaptation can be achieved. Without this knowledge it would be possible to train the wrong energy system for a particular sport and hinder or curtail positive adaptation.

Energy pathway is the term given to the chain of events that enables the body to produce energy. There are three energy pathways available to the body: aerobic, immediate anaerobic and short-term anaerobic.

The Aerobic Energy Pathway

Aerobic literally means 'with air'. Oxygen provides the catalyst for a chemical reaction in the muscles (including the heart) that generates aerobic energy (*see also* 'Krebs Cycle' and 'Lactate and Glycolysis', pages 5–6). If it were not for other factors such as insufficient muscular fuel sources (notably glycogen, *see* page 7), overheating and dehydration, the human body could theoretically continue to exercise aerobically indefinitely. (Endurance training is described in detail in part 6, where the crucial role of the brain in influencing endurance potential is discussed.)

Aerobic workouts are also called 'steady state' because the body's energy demands are balanced by energy supply, allowing exercise to be continued – hence the steady state. When the steady state is breached, such as by an increase in exercise intensity (a consequence of increased speed and/or distance, for example), the body will change the way it produces energy. It will do this with less oxygen, and energy will be produced anaerobically.

Sports Training Tip

Aerobic training provides base condition for most sports, regardless of their specific energy pathway demands. A good foundation of aerobic fitness will enable a sprinter (who relies predominantly on the immediate anaerobic pathway) to recover more quickly between efforts, and a football midfielder to sustain the high energy output required across the 90 minutes or more of a match (a sport which relies more on the short-term anaerobic energy pathway). It should be noted that certain sports require more aerobic fitness than others. Table 1.1 provides a breakdown of the aerobic and anaerobic components of selected track and field events and other sports.

Sports Training Tip

Aerobic training increases the body's ability to mobilise fat as an energy source at sub-maximal intensities, as well as improving carbohydrate metabolism. This will significantly improve the 'range' of the endurance athlete.

Anaerobic Energy Pathways

Anaerobic literally means 'without oxygen'. The body can create anaerobic energy in two ways, through the:

1 **immediate anaerobic** energy pathway;
2 and the **short-term anaerobic** energy pathway.

Neither pathway provides sustainable energy for very long.

The Immediate Anaerobic Energy Pathway

The immediate anaerobic pathway does not rely on oxygen to sustain it. It supplies energy that lasts no more than six to eight seconds. Although all sports activity is fuelled by stored 'high energy' chemicals such as adenosine triphosphate (ATP) and creatine phosphate (CP) (of which more later) and a chemical reaction that 'fires' them up, the immediate anaerobic energy pathway has a very short-lived, intense use of them.

Athlete and coach should think of the immediate anaerobic energy pathway as being like an explosion, where an incredible amount of energy is released in a very short time. From this analogy it becomes apparent that this is the energy pathway of choice for 'explosive' athletes, such as power lifters, weightlifters and sprinters. Too much aerobic training can dull this explosiveness and stifle fast twitch muscle fibre adaptation.

A tennis serve, power clean, long jump or 40m sprint are prime examples of the immediate anaerobic system in action.

Sports Training Tip

Aerobic fitness provides the foundation for the majority of all other types of fitness. Such a 'base' will enable athletes to recover more quickly between training exertions such as repeated sprints and weight-lifts.

The Short-term Anaerobic Energy Pathway

Like the immediate anaerobic energy pathway, the short-term anaerobic energy pathway also supplies the body with high-powered energy. However, it can provide energy for a little longer, up to around 90 seconds.

Under short-term anaerobic exercise conditions, such as 400m running, muscles will 'burn' (the result of increased lactate and the production of lactic acid, *see* page 125), and the heart will reach maximum output. These physiological reactions result from the body (and its muscles in particular) demanding more and more oxygen but not getting it.

The process of the body generating energy through the short-term anaerobic pathway is akin to running a car down a hill, turning the engine off and letting it attempt to climb a further hill. Sooner or later during the climb, power will completely run out and the car will stop and begin to roll back or, in the case of the athlete, grind to a halt.

As short-term anaerobic energy production passes the 20-second mark, more and more demand is placed on oxygen as a fuel source. After 30 seconds, 20 per cent of the energy produced is done so aerobically, and after 60 seconds this rises to 30 per cent. As the one-and-a-half minute mark is reached, no

amount of oxygen gulping will save the anaerobic 'engine', and it and the athlete will ultimately grind to a potentially painful halt.

Sports Training Tip

Training the anaerobic energy pathways will increase the body's ability to replenish the high-energy phosphates used to create energy. This will in turn extend athletes' ability to produce more high-powered efforts, as long as adequate rest is allowed (*see also* 'Creatine Supplementation, page 201).

Lactate and Glycolysis

Like many athletes and coaches, I was brought up on the notion that the body chemical lactate (particularly as lactic acid) was 'bad'. After all, why would we want to warm down to clear our muscles of it if it was good? It was a 'waste' product that potentially caused muscle damage and was the sole consequence of anaerobic training. However, lactate (and lactic acid) is in fact a crucial element in energy production for exercise of both short and long duration.

Lactate is produced in muscles at very low exercise intensities as well as at much higher ones, and is actually present in the body at rest. Lactate levels increase as exercise intensity rises in response to glycolysis – literally meaning 'the breaking down of glucose'. Glucose derives from carbohydrate consumption. Glycolysis kick-starts chemical processes within muscles that produce the energy required for sustained muscular contractions. Without glycolysis, exercise could not last for more than a few seconds.

There are two types of glycolysis: *oxygen dependent* and *oxygen independent* (these can be equated to the aerobic and anaerobic pathways). Each produces lactate, although the latter produces lactic acid (just how will be covered later).

Table 1.1	Selected Track and Field Events and Sports and their Respective Energy Pathway Requirements	
Event	Aerobic energy pathway contribution	Anaerobic energy pathway contribution
200m	5%	95%
800m	34%	66%
1,500m	50%	50%
10,000m	80%	20%
Marathon	98%	2%
Baseball		100%
Basketball		100%
Football:		
goalkeeper		100%
forward		100%
midfielder	20%	60%
Field hockey	20%	80%

Pyruvic Acid

The breakdown of glucose results in the production of pyruvic acid (PA). Over 10 different chemical reactions are involved in this process. PA is then used within the Krebs cycle (*see* below). When PA begins to accumulate in muscles, through what can be a relatively small increase in exercise intensity, the enzyme lactic dehydrogenase converts it to lactate. Under moderate to high exercise intensities, lactate is converted back to PA and reused to continue producing energy. At high exercise intensities, however, muscles are unable to do this and lactate production outstrips PA production. The result is that exercise becomes increasingly difficult and lactic acid is formed.

The production of lactic acid and its effect on performance is covered in more detail on page 125.

The Krebs Cycle and ATP

The Krebs cycle provides nearly 90 per cent of the energy required for aerobic exercise and produces adenosine triphosphate (ATP), an energy-rich compound. Energy for fuelling the body does not come directly from the food we consume; rather, ATP produces the energy (along with other energy-releasing phosphates). It provides muscular power under aerobic and anaerobic energy conditions and is known as the body's universal energy donor as oxygen is not required for its energy to be released from cells. The Krebs cycle permits the regeneration of ATP under aerobic conditions. During the Krebs cycle, PA changes to a form of acetic acid, which breaks down carbohydrate (glucose and glycogen) via the release of carbon dioxide and hydrogen ions to produce aerobic energy and ATP within the working muscles.

Endurance training will increase the number

of enzymes relevant to the Krebs cycle. Their numbers may actually be increased two- to threefold after a sustained period of this training.

The body's cells can store only limited amounts of ATP (about 85g at any one time). Therefore it has to be constantly re-synthesised. Muscles are able to store creatine phosphate in greater amounts (*see* below).

Creatine Phosphate (CP)

Creatine phosphate, like ATP, is a high-energy compound that does not require oxygen to ignite it. Even when combined, ATP and CP can only sustain flat-out effort for five to eight seconds as they provide fuel for the immediate anaerobic energy pathway.

Approximately 5 millimoles (mmol) of ATP and 15mmol of CP are stored within 1kg of muscle.

Creatine Supplementation and Sports Performance

Creatine is a sports supplement that can boost immediate and short-term anaerobic power. This is achieved by 'loading' muscles with a greater creatine concentration. This allows the athlete to handle increased training loads, resulting in greater strength and power and speed gains. Basically, creatine supplementation puts more 'high octane' fuel into the power athlete's tank (see page 201 for more detail on creatine supplementation).

Glycogen

Glycogen is also premium grade muscle fuel, converted in the body from carbohydrate (*see* page 186). It can be stored in the muscles and liver in limited amounts (on average around 375g). It is argued that a tough two-hour endurance workout would virtually deplete the liver and muscles of glycogen reserves. Consequently, glycogen must be replenished via optimum carbohydrate consumption (*see* page 186–7). A carefully constructed training programme that includes rest days and training of varying intensity will also maximise glycogen replenishment. Liver glycogen stores, although small, are crucial as they fuel the brain as well as the muscles during exercise. Liver glycogen becomes glucose during exercise. If the liver fails to meet glucose demands then the athlete will feel faint/light-headed and weak. This condition is called hypoglycaemia. Nutritional strategies for avoiding this are covered in part 10.

It takes about an hour to restock 5 per cent of the body's glycogen stores, assuming optimal carbohydrate consumption.

What Happens when Glycogen Stores Decrease?

When glycogen stores run down, endurance athletes 'hit the wall'. They will feel incredibly fatigued and light-headed, and their bodies may switch significantly to using fat and even protein as energy sources. However, the trained endurance athlete is much more adept at using fat as an energy source. This offsets their glycogen usage, pushing their endurance forwards.

Protein as an energy source has a catabolic effect. Basically, this means that the body begins to 'eat' itself to supply energy. This sounds drastic, and in many ways it is, as valuable lean muscle will be lost as the body searches for fuel and obtains it from its muscles. Consequently, endurance athletes need to 'think' protein as much as carbohydrate when it comes to their nutrition. It is now argued that the most successful post-workout energy replacement strategy is one that involves protein (and carbohydrate) replenishment (*see* page 188).

Metabolic Rate

Metabolic rate basically refers to the energy released by the body to power all the processes that keep it alive. Athletic training can have a significant effect on metabolic rate (see page 196). Metabolic rate comprises:

- **Total daily energy expenditure (TDEE):** This is the total of all the energy the body burns over a day.
- **Resting metabolic rate (RMR):** A very significant proportion (60–75 per cent) of TDEE is used to maintain RMR. RMR encompasses all those essential bodily functions we take for granted, such as heart, lung and mental functioning. Calculations of RMR are made over a 24-hour period, but do not include the calories burned while sleeping.
- **Thermic effect of feeding (TEF):** The process of eating and digesting food burns around 10 per cent of TDEE.
- **Activity:** Actual physical exertion accounts for only about 15 per cent of TDEE, although this can have a very significant effect on weight loss, weight gain and body composition.

Table 1.2 provides a guide to calculating the calories burned during various sports and types of exercise. It will help athlete and coach calculate calorific expenditure. However, the effect of sports training on metabolic rate should also be factored into the equation – training can increase metabolic rate (and therefore calorific expenditure) by as much as 20 per cent (*see* page 196).

Note

- Weights and plyometric exercises burn approximately 5–8 calories per minute dependent on body weight and exercise intensity.
- Calorie counters on heart rate monitors provide only an estimate of energy expenditure.

Table 1.2	Energy Expenditure and Exercise – Calories Burned Per Minute							
Activity	Kg	59	62	65	68	71	74	77	80
Volleyball		3.0	3.1	3.3	3.4	3.6	3.7	3.9	4.0
Easy cycling		5.9	6.2	6.5	6.8	7.1	7.4	7.7	8.0
Tennis		6.4	6.8	7.1	7.4	7.7	8.1	8.4	8.7
Easy swimming		7.6	7.9	8.3	8.7	9.1	9.5	9.9	10.2
Running at 8 min/mile pace		12.5	13.1	13.6	14.2	14.8	15.4	16.0	16.5

Adapted from W. McArdle, F. Katch and V. Katch, *Essentials of exercise physiology*, Williams and Wilkins, 1994

Understanding Food Energy

A Kcal and a Calorie supply the same amount of energy (which is why the terms can be used interchangeably).
Metric: 1 Kcal = 1000 cal
Imperial: 1 Calorie = 1000 c

1 cal is the amount of heat required to increase the temperature of 1 gram (g) of water by 1 degree centigrade. It is a very small amount of energy, hence the general use of the bigger Kcal unit.

Sports Training Tip

It is crucial that athlete and coach realise that fundamental conditioning 'theories' and processes must be adapted specifically for individual athletes. Age, training maturity, time of the training year, the way an individual's body responds to training and previous injuries must all be factored into the sports coaching/conditioning equation if optimum results are to be achieved. No two athletes will have exactly the same training needs. Coaches of groups of athletes take note.

Muscles

Muscles convert chemical energy, such as ATP and CP, into mechanical (sports and everyday) movement.

There are more than 430 voluntary muscles and over 250 million muscle fibres in the body. Muscle fibres are bundles of cells, which are held together by collagen (connective tissue). Each fibre consists of a membrane, numerous nuclei and thousands of myofibrils (inner strands) that run the length of the fibre. In order to perform sports skills, numerous muscles and muscle fibres interact. These are 'controlled' via messages sent from the brain through the spinal cord and out to the muscles.

When these electrical signals reach the muscles they are translated into chemical energy and the muscles contract. Specifically, the anterior motor neuron receives the electrical signal and muscle motor units and muscle fibres perform the mechanical action in consequence of the chemical reaction. Depending on the activity and the chemical reaction, this muscular action can be short-lived or longer lasting, aerobic and anaerobic.

Motor units are like a car engine's starter motor, while the brain is the key. The former kicks muscle fibres into action (or rather more accurately 'contraction') after the latter has been turned.

Some muscles have large numbers of motor units and low numbers of fibres. This enables them to execute highly precise movements. The eye, for example, has one motor unit for every 10 muscle fibres. This contrasts with other body parts that perform larger, much more powerful movements, such as the thigh and calf muscles. As an example, the gastrocnemius (calf muscle) has 580 motor units to 1.3 million fibres.

The interaction that occurs at muscular (tendon and joint) level is two-way. Various feedback and control mechanisms are in-built to prevent muscles from damaging themselves by over-contracting. These *proprioceptive* components of motor units, joints and ligaments continually monitor muscular stretch. They swing into action if, for example, a limb is moved beyond its normal range of movement (ROM). This is achieved by muscle spindles 'pulling back' on muscle fibres to reduce the stretch. This stretch/reflex is a vital component of the body's muscular safety mechanism, but it also plays a significant role in developing greater fast twitch (dynamic) muscle power through plyometric muscular action (*see* page 12 and part 5).

Muscular Adaptation

Muscles respond to training in response to *overload*; simply put, this means that when they are subjected to a load, effort or level of intensity with which they are not familiar, they respond by gaining in strength, size, power or increased repetition capacity (endurance performance). The increase in muscular strength can be accompanied by a noticeable increase in size (muscular *hypertrophy*). Fast twitch muscle fibre and, in particular, type IIb fibre (of which more later) has the greatest potential for actual visible changes in size.

Muscular Adaptation and Endurance Training

Endurance athletes and coaches should note that relevant training-induced changes in muscle play a highly significant role in improving endurance. Muscles will respond by increasing their number of capillaries, thus increasing oxygenated blood flow (capillaries can be likened to oxygen-carrying highways). Muscle fibre will also become better at producing the sustained chemical reactions responsible for aerobic (and anaerobic) energy metabolism, for example by boosting lactate/lactic tolerance. All muscle fibre types can improve their level of oxygen processing. Additionally, *mitochondria* (cellular power plants) will become better at generating ATP aerobically.

What do Muscles Contain?

Around 75 per cent of skeletal muscle is water, 20 per cent is protein and 5 per cent comprises inorganic salts and other elements, including the high-energy phosphates ATP and CP. Protein is the key to building stronger muscles.

An athlete is a product of how they train. The 'right' energy systems and muscle fibres have to be trained if their maximum, or near maximum, potential is to be achieved.

Types of Muscle Fibre

Not all muscle fibres are the same, as they are designed to carry out different energy-releasing functions. Some are suited to powerful explosive movements, like sprinting and weight-training (fast twitch muscle fibre), while others are suited to longer-duration activities, like rowing, walking and running (slow twitch muscle fibre). These fibre types are fairly evenly distributed throughout the body at birth.

Slow Twitch Type I Fibre

Type I fibres are designed to sustain relatively slow but long-lived muscular contractions. They are also known as slow twitch, red or slow oxidative (SO) fibres, as they function for long periods on aerobic energy. They twitch at a rate of 10–30 per second.

Fast Twitch Type II Fibre

Fast twitch muscle fibres contract two to three times faster than slow twitch muscle fibres, producing 30–70 twitches per second. These fibres are also known as white fibres.

There are two basic types of fast twitch fibre:

Table 1.3	Summary of Energy Pathways, Muscle Fibre and Sports Training			
Energy pathway	Reliance on oxygen*/energy source	Duration	Selected sports activities using energy pathway	Effects of training pathway
Immediate anaerobic	No reliance on oxygen. Relies on stored energy sources (ATP, CP) in muscles and a chemical reaction that releases their energy.	6–8 sec	Weightlifting, sprints from 10–40m, gymnastic vaults, athletic field events	Improves availability of stored energy sources, e.g. CP. Targets fast twitch muscle fibre, particularly type IIb, and can increase muscle size.
Short-term anaerobic	Relies on a mix of stored chemicals (ATP and CP) and oxygen. Oxygen can never be supplied in sufficient quantities to sustain the energy produced (also supplies energy to endurance activities when steady state is breached).	6–90 sec	400m running and stop/start activities like martial arts, racket sports, football, rugby and circuit training	Targets type IIa and type IIb fast twitch muscle fibre and improves their speed, endurance and power
Aerobic energy	Relies on oxygen transport to the working muscles via the heart and lungs and an ensuing chemical reaction to sustain muscular action (Krebs cycle/ oxygen-dependent glycolysis)	If it were not for other factors, such as lack of food, overheating and dehydration, our bodies could theoretically continue to exercise aerobically indefinitely	Marathon running, triathlon, distance cycling and other ultra-distance events. Note: Aerobic fitness provides the foundation for the immediate and the short-term anaerobic energy pathways, serving as a general base on which they can be developed	Targets type I slow twitch muscle fibre and significantly enhances its oxygen-processing capability

Note: In reality, most sports are fuelled by an amalgamation of all energy pathways (see Table 1.1).

- **Type IIa:** Type IIa or 'intermediate' fast twitch fibres are also termed fast oxidative glycotic (FOG) because of their ability to display, when subject to the relevant training stimuli, a relatively high capacity to contract under conditions of aerobic or anaerobic energy production.
- **Type IIb:** Type IIb fibres act as 'turbo-chargers' in muscles. They swing into action for high-powered activity, such as a 40m sprint. These fibres are also known as fast glycogenolytic (FG) fibres. They rely almost exclusively on the immediate anaerobic energy pathway to fire them up.

Fast twitch muscle fibre requires a particularly strong mental input to fully recruit it. Fast twitch bundles of fibres (motor units) actually recruit according to their size; the largest, most powerful ones need great mental stimulation to be called into action (*see* part 9 for relevant mental training tips).

Are Speed Athletes Born Fast?

It is often thought that those blessed with great speed or strength are born with a higher percentage of fast twitch muscle fibres, and that no amount of speed training or power training will 'turn a carthorse into a racehorse'. Although this may be true within certain parameters, the distribution of fast twitch muscle fibres is actually fairly even in the muscles of sedentary people. Most possess 45–55 per cent of fast twitch fibres and 45–55 per cent of slow twitch fibres. This is an important consideration when searching for athletic talent. The path towards a speed or power-orientated sport (or endurance one) does reflect genetics to a certain degree, but more pertinent for the majority is dependent on:

1. the way sporting experiences are shaped at a relatively early age;
2. how muscle fibres are trained throughout a sporting career.

Table 1.4	Fast Twitch Muscle Percentages in Selected Sports Activities Compared to Sedentary Individuals (and a Very Speedy Animal!)
Individual	Percentage fast twitch muscle fibre
Sedentary	45–55%
Distance runner	25%
Middle-distance runner	35%
Sprinter	84%
Cheetah	83% of the total number of fibres examined in the rear outer portion of the thigh (vastus lateralis) and nearly 61% of the gastrocnemius were comprised of fast twitch fibres

Adapted from Golink 73 (in F.W. Dick, *Sports Training Principles*, fourth edition, A&C Black, 2002, page 109) and Williams (*J. Comp. Physiol.* [B], 1997 Nov; 167(8):527–35)

Training-induced Changes in Muscle Fibre

Muscle fibre can be 'changed' when subject to a constant training stimulus. Fast twitch muscle fibre, for example, can be made faster and more powerful. Whether these changes are lasting when training is stopped is debatable. Current research indicates that fast twitch fibres are likely to become permanently 'slowed' by endurance training – speed athletes and coaches take note. More information on muscle fibre adaptation is found in parts 6 and 8.

One of the few studies to concern itself with the long-term effects of endurance training was conducted by Thayer and associates. The team looked at muscle fibre adaptation over a decade. Skeletal muscle from seven subjects who had participated in 10 years or more of high-intensity aerobic training (DT) and six non-trained (NT) subjects was obtained by muscle biopsy from the vastus lateralis muscle (a thigh muscle that extends the knee).

The percentage of slow twitch fibres in the DT group was 70.9, compared to 37.7 in the NT group. In terms of fast twitch fibres, the DT group's percentage stood at 25.3, which compared to 51.8 with the NT controls. The researchers concluded that endurance training may promote a transition from type II to type I muscle fibre types and that this occurs at the expense of the type II fibre population. (Reference: *J. Sports Med. Phys. Fitness*, 2000 Dec; 40(4):284–9)

The implication for coaches and athletes is that the 'right' training will positively affect muscle fibre change for sport.

Types of Muscular Contraction

It is important for athlete and coach to understand how muscles physically contract to create force and movement, as this has crucial implications when training muscles to develop sport-specific strength and power.

Isotonic Muscular Action

Isotonic muscular action involves movement and incorporates 'concentric' and 'eccentric' actions (*see* below). Curling and lowering a dumbbell (when performing a biceps curl) and running are examples of isotonic muscular actions.

Concentric Muscular Action

A concentric action involves a muscle shortening as it contracts to create movement or apply force. It is the most common direction of effort for sport. During a biceps curl, for example, the biceps muscle contracts concentrically to raise the dumbbell.

Eccentric Muscular Action

An eccentric muscular action involves a muscle lengthening as it contracts. During the biceps curl, for example, the biceps muscle works eccentrically as the weight is lowered. Although coaches and athletes do not always realise this, eccentric muscle contractions are crucial to sports performance. For instance, numerous eccentric contractions take place while running, in the calf, thigh and hip muscles on foot strike.

Plyometric Muscular Action

Plyometric exercises and movements are very dynamic. Hopping and depth jumps are typical examples. Plyometric exercises work on the principle that a concentric muscular contraction is much stronger if it immediately follows an eccentric contraction of the same muscle. It is a bit like stretching out a coiled spring to its fullest extent and then letting it go: immense levels of energy will be released in a split second as the spring recoils. Plyometric exercises develop this recoil or, more technically, the 'stretch/reflex' capacity in a muscle. Running is a plyometric activity, regardless of speed. Plyometric conditioning methods are covered in part 5.

Isokinetic Muscular Action

Isokinetic muscular action involves moving a preset resistance (concentrically and/or eccentrically) over a full or part range of movement – the weight cannot be accelerated, as is usually the case with free and fixed weights. Isokinetic resistance training machines exist in some gyms, although the majority of fixed-weight installations are isotonic. Isokinetic machines are often used for injury rehabilitation purposes. Isokinetic movement is less relevant for directly improving sports performance.

Hormones, the Endocrine System and Sports Training

Physiologists refer to hormones as 'chemical messengers'. They are produced by the endocrine system and endocrine glands, such as the hypothalamus in the brain and the gonads. The major function of hormones is to change the rates of specific reactions in target cells. A cell's actual response to a hormone is determined by the presence of certain protein receptors in its membrane or interior. Muscle fibres, like the rest of the body, are constituted from cells, and the way a hormone interacts with these can significantly affect training adaptation. The hormonal contribution involves a complex physiological response, but ultimately results in the DNA-mediated synthesis of new contractile proteins, which are vital to muscle cell function and integrity.

DNA

DNA (deoxyribonucleic acid) is the blueprint of every living organism. Specifically, it is a highly specialised series of molecules (nucleic acids) found in the nuclei of all cells. DNA is transmitted across generations through reproduction. It can be 'read' and its code used for various genetic and forensic purposes.

Part 4, with its focus on weight-training, provides a more detailed examination of the important role of hormones (notably growth hormone and testosterone) when training for sport.

Adaptation and Rest

As noted, adaptation is the term used to describe the positive changes that occur when the body is consistently subjected to a regular training stimulus. Rest is as crucial to this process as the training itself. It is during the periods when the athlete is *not* training that positive physiological changes are made.

When an athlete is subjected to a particularly hard training session, such as a 100 per cent sprint session or tough weight or interval workout, around 48 hours of rest is needed for full regeneration and recovery. During this period, glycogen stores are replenished, muscle protein is restored and 'new' muscle is built. This does not necessarily mean that no training should take place; rather that workout intensities should be reduced. The next intense session (or competition) should then be scheduled to take place 48 to 72 hours after the first intense workout to maximise training adaptation in a cyclical fashion. These principles apply whatever your age or sport, and allow for what is known as 'overcompensation'. This condition results in the body maximising its potential for peak physiological output at that time in the training plan. It is the continued use of these overcompensation periods that optimises the conditions for training progression (for more information, *see* part 8).

> Note: Competitions, with their increased mental requirements, are more draining than training sessions. Consequently, coach and athlete should carefully consider their placement in the athlete's competitive cycle.

Young and Master Athletes and the Sports Life Cycle

Although the prime years for athletic involvement in most sports are the late teens to early to mid-30s, sports training can still take place outside this window. Children may involve themselves in structured sports activities from the age of eight, and 'masters' can continue competing in age-graded competition in certain sports, such as athletics and indoor rowing, for as long as they care to do so.

Whatever the age of the athlete, young or old, training must be adapted to account for *physiological maturity*. It would obviously be inappropriate to give a 12-year-old the same training programme as a 28-year-old Olympian. Likewise, it would be inadvisable for a 58-year-old to attempt to train like the 28-year-old.

Training Maturity

Training maturity should also be considered. This refers to the number of years that an athlete has been training for their sport/event. A 26-year-old rugby player who has been training since his mini-rugby days at age 11 will be vastly more training mature than a 20-year-old who took up the sport at college and has one season of training behind him.

Training maturity will influence:

- the type and intensity of training that the athlete can handle;
- the athlete's bank of appropriate skills (and their ability to pick up new ones);
- the physiological responsiveness of the athlete's body;
- the athlete's mental readiness, motivation and focus.

The Younger Athlete

There are times when the developing body is more susceptible to certain types of training than others (*see* Tables 1.5 and 1.6). The coach also needs to be aware of *growth spurts* in a young athlete's life when they will, for example, be less coordinated due to the way their body and limbs are growing. Likewise, there are windows of opportunity when the young athlete's mind is ripe for learning sports skills (called *skill windows*). For boys, this skill window occurs between the ages of 6 and 12; for girls it is between the ages of 5 or 6 and 11.

These skill windows should be regarded as the best opportunity to place into the child's physical skills memory the key components of general, rather than specific, sports skills. Specialisation for most sports should be avoided until the mid- to late teens. During this 'learning to train' phase, the basics of running, jumping, throwing and agility skills should be mastered. Skill acquisition is covered in detail in part 9.

Sports Training Tip

If basic sports skill (physical literacy) is not learned during the young athlete's skill window period, it is unlikely that the athlete will ever reach their full potential.

Coaches should not treat children as mini-adults. Rather, they should train and talk to them appropriately (see page 211).

FUNdaMENTAL refers to the period when the child is most susceptible to developing physical literacy.

Table 1.5	Critical Development Windows in the Young Athlete – Boys				
Age	Stages	Skill	Speed	Strength	Endurance (aerobic)
6		Skill window	Speed window 1		
7	FUNdaMENTAL				
8					
9	Learning to train				
10					
11			Speed window 2		
12					
13	Training to			Strength window	Aerobic window
14					
15					
16	Training to				
17					
18					
19	Training to win				
20					
21					

Table adapted from UK athletics coaches' education programme.

Table 1.6 — Critical Development Windows in the Young Athlete – Girls

Age	Stages	Skill	Speed	Strength	Endurance (aerobic)
6					
7	FUNdaMENTAL		Speed window		
8		Skill window 1			
9	Learning to				
10	train				
11					
12					
13					
14	Training to train		Speed window 2	Strength window	Aerobic window
15					
16	Training to				
17	compete				
18					
19	Training to win				
20					
21					

Table adapted from UK athletics coaches' education programme.

Note: The information provided is for guidance only. No two children will mature at exactly the same rate. The windows identified should not be seen as the only time to develop these qualities; rather they should be regarded as the most fertile times to develop these physical attributes. Progress, though not so great, can be made at other times.

Long-term Athletic Development

Long-term athletic development (LTD) is vital if the athlete is to arrive at their peak competitive years in prime condition. Coaches should use as a guide the average ages for peak performance of elite performers in their sport/event/position, and lead the athlete towards achieving success at this time. Obviously, there will be exceptions, and athletes will 'mature' earlier and later.

Training the Master Athlete

The number of athletes competing in masters sports is on the increase. In sports such as swimming, indoor rowing and athletics, competitions are regularly held at regional, national, European and world level. Most have competitions in designated age bands (usually five years), enabling athletes to compete against their peers. Regardless of age, incredible performances are still achievable, although there will inevitably be some physiological decline. The major reasons for this decline are identified below.

Overview of Reasons for Age-related Decline in Physiological Sports Performance

- **Decline in muscle mass and muscle fibre.** The body will experience a 10 per cent decline in muscle mass between the ages of 25 and 50, and a further 45 per cent by the eighth decade – if nothing is done about it. To put this into context, the biceps muscle of a newborn baby has around 500,000 fibres, while that of an 80-year-old has only about 300,000. With decreased muscle mass comes reduced strength, speed and power capability.

- **Less growth hormone (GH).** One of the major consequences of a reduction in growth hormone production is a diminished level of protein synthesis. As protein is the key building block for muscle, this also leads to muscle shrinkage (atrophy).

- **Decline in fast twitch muscle fibre.** Fast twitch muscle fibre declines much faster than slow twitch fibre with age – by as much as 30 per cent between the ages of 20 and 80. This is because the nerves that control these fibres die off, with knock-on consequences for the fibres themselves.

- **Reduced production of creatine phosphate.** As noted, creatine phosphate is crucial for short-duration physical activity. Production of this chemical declines with age. With less of it in the muscles, the older athlete can become less able to tackle high-intensity interval workouts.

- **Reduced flexibility.** With age, soft tissue (muscles, ligaments and tendons) hardens and joints stiffen, which increases the potential for injury.
- **Aerobic capacity.** A 1 per cent drop in maximal aerobic capacity (VO2max) for every year that passes after 25 is the norm for sedentary people (*see* page 120 for more information on VO2max).

All the above factors can be positively challenged with appropriate training.

Sports Training Tip

Master athletes should use the same techniques as their more youthful counterparts to develop and maintain their condition, but they must be mindful of the stresses that certain types of training can place on their older bodies. Pre-conditioning (see part 2) is a must, as it is for all athletes.

Should Women Train Differently From Men?

The basic answer is no – women will respond physiologically to training in the same way as men. As an example, women can become as strong as men on a percentage basis, accounting for their smaller stature and amount of muscle. However, there are some factors that need to be accounted for when coaching the female athlete. For example, the structure of the female body affects the knee joint, specifically the ante-rior cruciate ligament (ACL) of the knee (*see* page 33). Other issues to consider are stress fractures (*see* below) and women's general and hormonal response to sports and exercise. Additional comment is made on training female athletes with regard to their nutritional needs (*see* page 191).

Stress Fractures in Women

Women can be up to 12 times more likely than men to suffer stress fractures when subject to the same training. A stress fracture is a minute crack in a bone that can be very difficult to detect by x-ray. The runner will be unable to run and will experience localised leg pain. Stress fractures are caused by high mileages, running in inappropriate shoes and on hard surfaces, and because of female-specific issues, such as hormonal response that affects bone strength.

Tips to Avoid Stress Fractures (for Men and Women)

- Maintain calcium intake to RDA levels (700–1000mg).
- Eat a balanced, nutritionally rich diet. Research indicates that female athletes with stress fractures are often on nutritionally restricted diets.
- Women should monitor their menstrual cycle. Research indicates that if their cycle reduces to six or less a year (a potential consequence of regular intense training) then they are six times more likely to suffer stress fractures.

PART **TWO**

PRE-CONDITIONING FOR INJURY-FREE TRAINING

Sports scientists and coaches have recently developed the concept of 'pre-conditioning' (also known as pre-training) as a means of reducing athlete injury and improving sports performance. Essentially, pre-conditioning means 'training to train'. During pre-conditioning workouts, the emphasis is placed on protecting and strengthening body parts that are prone to injury in order to increase their tolerance and sports readiness. It is akin to laying strong foundations for a complex building; without the former there is little chance of the latter remaining standing.

When is the Right Time to Pre-condition?

The start of the training year might seem the ideal time to pre-condition. Indeed, numerous coaches might argue that they already do this by emphasising general training methods (to build a foundation of strength for more specific work) in the early stages of training. General training methods are those that do not closely match the sport being trained for. As an example, circuit training (*see* page 77) would develop preparatory condition for a cricketer. However, pre-conditioning is more than just general exercise performed at the beginning of the training cycle. It should be much more exacting and a part of the athlete's year-round training (albeit, perhaps, with slightly reduced emphasis at certain times, such as when the competitive season approaches).Wherever possible, the exercises selected should have some form of synergy to the athlete's sport.

The best pre-conditioning programme carefully selects exercises and drills and matches them to the athlete – their age, prior injury history, competitive level and level of training maturity – as well as to the time of the training year/period.

Pre-conditioning Factors

Ultimately, pre-conditioning underpins all aspects of training. However, its effectiveness depends on a broad range of determining factors. Understanding these will enable athlete and coach to design the most effective training programme.

Muscular Action

Most sports rely on a combination of concentric and eccentric muscular actions (*see* part 1). However, it is eccentric contractions that create more muscular soreness and damage in both the short and long term.

Many runners will, for example, be familiar with the 'delayed onset of muscle soreness' (DOMS) that occurs in the thighs after a workout involving downhill runs. This results from the quadriceps (front thigh muscles) having to stretch on ground strike to control the speed of the descent (an eccentric contraction).

The 'absorption as stretch' part of the eccentric contraction has been identified as the greatest factor in creating potential soft tissue strain (*see* pages 23 and 29 for examples of eccentric training methods as ways of combating strain). The Achilles tendons are particularly prone to eccentric damage from downhill running.

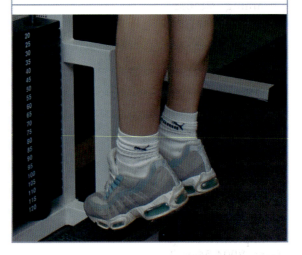

Figure 2.1 Eccentric Calf Raise to Pre-condition Achilles Tendons

Learning from Previous Injuries

Minimising injury is crucial to pre-conditioning. However, if an athlete *does* sustain an injury it is important to understand why and take remedial steps to avoid a recurrence. This process must form a significant part of future pre-conditioning programmes. In this respect, self-diagnostic tests can be used throughout the training period to predict potential injury (*see* Table 2.2).

The coach must also ensure that the athlete does not 'forget' to perform their designated pre-conditioning exercises if these are done away from main training workouts and the coach's watchful gaze. Athletes are notorious for neglecting pre-conditioning/remedial exercises (the latter perhaps administered by a physiotherapist) once they 'feel' that they have recovered from an injury. The athlete should continue to include these exercises in their training routines to minimise potential injury recurrence.

Researchers have investigated hamstring injuries in elite athletes, hypothesising that athletes with a prior history of hamstring muscle strain were at increased risk of sustaining similar injuries in future. The research involved nine athletes with a history of unilateral hamstring injury and eighteen uninjured subjects. Using specialised equipment, the researchers compared the torque that the hamstring muscles were able to exert (torque is a force that produces a twisting or rotating aspect – muscular torque creates greater potential for strain). The researchers found that torque peaked at much shorter muscle lengths in the injured athletes than the non-injured, and recommended that to prevent further injury a combined programme of muscle testing and eccentric exercises should be implemented. (Reference: *Med. Sci. Sports Exerc.*, 2004 Mar; 36(3):379–87.)

Implications for Coaches

Not all coaches have access to equipment like the isokinetic machinery required to test muscular strength (*see* part 1), but this should not be seen as a huge impediment to successful pre-conditioning (and injury prevention) as there are numerous other methods available:

- **Use 'home-grown' tests to determine muscular weaknesses and imbalances.** For example, one-repetition weight-training maximums (1RM) and/or plyometric (jumping) bests can provide much useful information. These can also be used as periodic points of reference during the full training programme. If, for example, an athlete displays a significant discrepancy in strength between legs, then the coach can instigate training designed to promote greater balance. In so doing, they will also increase an athlete's general ability to express power, potentially improving sports performance as well as reducing injury risk.
- **Develop a repertoire of relevant pre-conditioning exercises – and know when to use them.** Selected examples of pre-conditioning exercises are offered in Table 2.3. Weight-training as a pre-conditioner is covered in more detail on pages 26–8.
- **Establish 'norms' for required sport-specific range of movement (SSROM).** Injury is likely if insufficient SSROM is available in key muscle and tendon groups, such as the hamstrings and Achilles tendons for sprinters. This process will be subjective to some extent, particularly for athletes of low training maturity. However, the process of working out where muscular tightness could at best impair performance and at worse lead to injury is key to successful pre-conditioning.

Sport-specific Range of Movement (SSROM)

SSROM refers to the specific movement that the athlete's muscles and joints pass through in order to perform their sport skill optimally.

For example, the hamstring muscles of a sprinter have to move from relatively constrained positions through to extended ones. The sprint action is of course performed at maximum speed and generates great torque and force. Consequently, SSROM becomes crucial as it allows, in this case, the sprint action to be performed effectively, safely and with minimum injury risk. Numerous drills can be employed by coach/athlete to condition SSROM.

Sports Training Tip

SSROM differs from range of movement (ROM). The former describes the amount of joint movement required to perform a sports skill optimally and the latter the full ROM available to the athlete. ROM could actually be greater than SSROM. However, in some cases possessing too much ROM can be a hindrance as it can slow the performance of dynamic, short, sharp movements.

Table 2.1	Indicators of Insufficient SSROM	
Insufficient SSROM indicator	Relevant sport/s	Selected SSROM developers
From a lying position the athlete is unable to lift and pull one leg back towards the body to a vertical position, while the other leg remains in contact with the ground	All sports	Lying hamstring stretch and leg cycling (see pages 48 and 46)
Inability to pull heel of one leg close to buttock when standing on the other leg	All sports	Standing quadriceps stretch, walking/running actions and leg cycling (see page 46)
Inability to press knee beyond toes, when one foot is extended in front of the other from a kneeling lunge-type position, without lifting heel of grounded foot	All running-based sports. This limitation indicates a tight Achilles tendon	The actual test makes a great stretch; hold the end position for 20 seconds after a suitable warm-up.
Inability to lift – or have lifted – both arms parallel to the ground behind the shoulders without excessive forward bending of upper body	Throwing sports and running	As above, the test makes a good stretch; hold at 'sticking point' for 15–20 seconds. Alternate arm swings

Analysing Sports Technique

From a pre-conditioning perspective, the emphasis should be on looking for muscular imbalances that can then be used to enhance performance. When filming a runner on a treadmill from behind, for example, the reviewer's eye should focus on hip alignment, the recovery phase of the running action, foot strike and back and shoulder position. From study of the film it may be possible to discern such problems as poor hamstring and hip flexor muscle strength (muscle at the top of the thigh), identified by a 'lazier' lower leg return phase* during the running cycle, or a lean on one side of the body which could lead to, for example, lower back injury. Coach and athlete can then design a training programme to counteract these technical deficiencies.

Self-testing for Potential Injury

Numerous self-diagnostic trigger point (TP) tests are available to coaches and athletes, although these should not be regarded as substitutes for expert sports medicine/physiotherapy interventions. TPs can flag up potential 'problems' before they become acute, allowing the coach/athlete an attempt to condition them out, ease back on training or seek appropriate professional help (*see* Table 2.2 below for a self-test for knee injury).

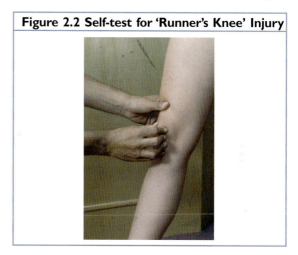

Figure 2.2 Self-test for 'Runner's Knee' Injury

Injury	Self-test	Method
Table 2.2 — Trigger Point Self-diagnostic Test to Identify Potential 'Runner's Knee'		
Patellofemoral pain syndrome (PFPS, commonly known as 'runner's knee') Symptoms: pain is normally on the outside of the knee and comes on after 20 minutes of running (see Table 2.3 for a potential treatment)	Palpating the kneecap	The coach uses their top hand to push down on the kneecap, lifting the lower pole of the patella. The thumb and forefinger of the lower hand then apply pressure to the lower borders of the inferior poles (sides) of the patella. If there is pain, it is more than likely that the athlete is suffering from/developing PFPS.

Adapted from T. Noakes, *The Lore of Running,* fourth edition, Human Kinetics, 2003

* The return phase of the running action occurs when the foot leaves the running surface and travels a curvilinear path under the body and through to a forward position for the next foot strike. *See* part 7 for a more detailed consideration of the (sprint) running action.

Using Eccentric Training Methods

As indicated, knowledge of muscular action is key to the coach's understanding of pre-conditioning. Eccentric drills and exercises can play a vital role.

Sample Eccentric Pre-conditioning Methods

- **For running:** Athlete completes 4 x 100m downhill efforts at 70 per cent of maximum speed as a prelude to faster downhill workouts. This will minimise residual soreness and the potential for more significant future strain.
- **All sports involving running, jumping and agility movements:** Perform eccentric exercises, such as 'drop and hold' depth jumps, where no attempt is made to spring back up from the jump on landing; rather the athlete just absorbs the impact, using a 'blocking' action with their legs. Depth jumps and other plyometric drills are covered in more detail in part 5.
- **Eccentric weight-training:** These lifts require the athlete to concentrate on the lowering phase of the exercise by, for example, controlling the weight as it is lowered to the chest during the bench press.

Eccentric exercise is not just a pre-conditioner; it is also a great training means, particularly for speed and power athletes as it has been shown to specifically target fast twitch muscle fibre.

Sports Training Tip

Weight-training is a pre-conditioning must since it can reduce the incidence of injury by strengthening soft tissue (of muscles, ligaments and tendons).

Endurance Athletes Should Weight-train

Endurance coaches and athletes should incorporate weight-training into their training programmes, even if they are wary of doing so from a performance-enhancing perspective. This will reduce potential for muscular strain and counter muscular imbalances.

Note: There can be 'complications' when training for endurance and power concurrently (see 'Training for Endurance and Weight-training – The Interference Effect', part 6, page 130). Circuit resistance training, where light weight exercises are performed over multiple repetitions and sets, makes a suitable exercise choice for the endurance athlete in this respect, especially if exercises relevant to the athlete's sport are selected.

Think beyond Immediate Power and Performance Strength Gains

Whatever the sport, coaches need to consider including muscle balancing exercises into their pre-conditioning and conditioning programmes. Coaches tend, quite naturally, to prefer exercises that have the capacity to develop their athlete's performance abilities. Invariably, they will look at how power is generated, for example, for a basketball jump shot or a tennis serve, and then design a progressive conditioning programme to enhance that capacity. Although this is obviously crucial for performance, thought must also be given to the muscles not directly involved in performing the relevant skill. Failure to do so could lead to muscular imbalances and potential injury. It is therefore vital for the coach to fully understand the muscular dynamics of all relevant sporting actions.

For example, shoulder and elbow problems often occur in racket sports players because of a necessary overemphasis on the 'hitting' muscles. Specifically, these athletes have very powerful internal shoulder rotation muscles and much weaker external rotators. The coach can address this by using balancing pre-conditioning exercises such as the cable external shoulder rotation, described below (*see also* page 29).

Sports Training Tip

Over-training is the term used by sports scientists to describe a state of staleness, fatigue and greater susceptibility to injury, which if not tackled can lead to injury, illness and performance decline. Strategies for combating over-training are covered in part 8. Over-reaching refers to a preliminary state of fatigue and potential injury risk.

Table 2.3 Selected Weight-training (and Other) Pre-conditioning Exercises			
Exercise	Pre-conditioning value	Sports applicability	Comments/tips
Leg extension (weights)	Stabilises and strengthens the knee joint, useful for combating knee problems, such as runner's knee and cruciate ligament strain	All	Suitable for independent left and right leg training for more balanced strength development
Backward running (body weight) Sideways running (body weight)	Improves agility, lower limb strength, flexibility and proprioception (the ability to perform a skill from an unstable position)	All running/jumping-based sports, as well as numerous others such as skiing and snowboarding	Can be included as a regular warm-up element
Eccentric calf raise	Strengthens Achilles tendons	All running-based sports	See page 29 for full description below

Table 2.3	Selected Weight-training (and Other) Pre-conditioning Exercises cont.		
Exercise	Pre-conditioning value	Sports applicability	Comments/tips
Cable external shoulder rotation	Balances shoulder strength	All hitting and throwing sports	See description below on page 29
Dynamic standing leg cycling	Develops concentric and eccentric hamstring strength, without the impact forces associated with running	All running sports	Stand tall and cycle one leg underneath the body in an out and back running action. Stand near a wall to aid balance. Increase speed as confidence develops.
Eccentric squats	Increases the shock absorbency (eccentric strength) of the thigh muscles and reduces injury risk	All running and jumping sports	Set up a Smith machine so that it allows the weight to be lowered under control. Have a training partner/coach on hand to assist if necessary.
Leg press	Reduces the risk of 'runner's knee' (PFPS, see page 25)	Running, particularly for endurance	Seek expert advice if exercise causes pain

Pre-conditioning Exercises

Combating Achilles Tendon Strain

'Tendinosis' is the technical term used to describe the degeneration of Achilles tendon tissue; Achilles tendinitis refers to inflammation of the soft tissue. Most Achilles pain is now believed to be a consequence of the former, particularly in training mature athletes.

Research indicates that heavy-load, eccentric calf-lowering exercises are a great way to treat Achilles tendon injury. Specifically, researchers focused on two matched groups of 15 recreational athletes, both suffering from long-term Achilles problems.

The first group performed the specific calf raises with an emphasis on the eccentric phase, while the other received 'normal' physiotherapy treatment. At the end of the 12-week training programme, the weight-training group were able to run at pre-injury levels. By contrast, the controls did not respond to physiotherapy and ultimately needed surgical treatment. (Reference: *Am. J. Sports Med.*, 1998, May-Jun; 26(3):360–6)

The Eccentric Calf Raise

The eccentric calf exercise is basically a normal calf raise, but with the emphasis placed on the lowering phase. The athlete concentrates on lowering the weights very slowly, perhaps to a slow four count. The resultant increase in eccentric strength in the lower legs places less strain on the tendons, as they and the calf muscles become more proficient at absorbing shock when running. Incidentally, this and other lower leg exercises, like straight-leg jumps (*see* page 96), improve force return on foot strike when running and jumping, thus increasing performance potential and reducing 'joint stiffness'. Basically, the muscular structures around the ankle become more resilient and powerful and 'naturally' able to return force.

Sample Pre-conditioning Routines

Although 'off-the-shelf' programmes, such as those that follow, have a useful educative purpose, they will not suit every athlete or every sport. Coach and athlete should be mindful of this and always strive to develop their own specific and relevant programmes.

The Cable External Shoulder Rotation

This is a pre-conditioning exercise for racket sports players. The athlete will need a training partner or their coach to assist them and a short medium-strength Dyna Band or similar rubber band exercise tube.

1 Stand in a 'ready' position with feet shoulder-width apart and left hand on hip.
2 A towel can be placed between the upper arm and side to act as a pivot and ensure the elbow is positioned directly below the shoulder.
3 Grasp the handle of the Dyna Band and flex the elbow to a 90-degree angle, holding the grip just in front and to the left of the navel.
4 The training partner should be positioned to the athlete's left, just behind them, with a firm grip on the other end of the Dyna Band (there must be tension in the band so that when the shoulder is externally rotated, the athlete pulls against a resistance).
5 The athlete rotates their shoulder externally (takes their hand away from their navel and out to the side) to stretch the Dyna Band. The lower arm should be kept parallel to the ground and the hand position held constant.

Table 2.4	Pre-conditioning Workout 1	
Suitable for: running-based sports, where sprinting is required.		Warm-up: 5–10 minutes of easy jogging
Exercise	**Repetitions**	**Comments**
Lunge walk	4 x 20m	
Leg cycling	4 x 20m	Increase speed as athlete progresses through the repetitions
High knee lift	4 x 20m	Increase speed as above
Foot drill	4 x 20m	Increase speed as above
Backward running	3 x 30m	Increase speed as above
Sideways skips	2 x 20m to left and right	Increase speed as above
Single-leg squats	3 x 10 on each leg	With body weight

Table 2.4	Pre-conditioning Workout 1 cont.	
Suitable for: running, but also designed to provide a level of base, local muscular endurance		Warm-up: 5–10 minutes of jogging or other suitable cardiovascular exercise
Exercise	**Duration/intensity**	**Comments**
Calf raises	3 × 20	Concentrate on the eccentric (lowering phase)
Hamstring bridge	3 × 6 10 – 20-second hold	With body weight
Medicine ball sit-up and throw	3 × 10 medium intensity	Do not perform at 100% effort as the athlete is preparing their body for greater power expression in future

The workout in table 2.5 is based on circuit training (CT) and circuit resistance training (CRT) (*see* part 4). The chosen exercises are particularly relevant to running-based sports. Coaches from other sports should select more specific exercises for their particular sport (*see* pages 80–2 for a description of CRT suitable for rowers). The number of circuits may depend on time spent in the training tier, the athlete's maturity or other factors.

Sports Training Tip

Although CT and CRT are great ways to develop strength endurance (see page 77) for those involved in endurance sports, they are also great pre-conditioners (and conditioners) for developing speed and agility, providing the coach selects the most appropriate exercises and ensures that technique is maintained.

Table 2.5	Pre-conditioning Workout 2	
Exercise	**Repetitions/duration**	**Comments/technique tips**
Press-up	30 sec on and off	Perform rhythmically

Table 2.5   Pre-conditioning Workout 2 cont.

Exercise	Repetitions/duration	Comments/technique tips
Hamstring bridge 	10 reps – hold for 2 sec	Try to keep relaxed and remember to breathe!
Sprint arm action 	20 sec on and off	Keep the shoulders down and maintain opposite leg-to-arm action
Sit-up 	30 sec on and off	Emphasise the contraction of the abdominal muscles when lifting the torso
Standing leg cycling 	20 reps each leg	Perform with controlled speed
Sit-up with twist 	30 sec on and off	Perform slowly; alternating left and right twists
Squat jumps 	15 jumps	Perform with controlled power and land light and quick on feet
Dumbbell bench press 	20 reps	Perform with control and symmetry – use a light to medium weight

Table 2.5	Pre-conditioning Workout 2 cont.	
Exercise	**Repetitions/duration**	**Comments/technique tips**
Straight leg jumps from side to side	30 sec on and off	Maintain a slight knee bend and land 'lightly' but quickly

Further Pre-conditioning Thoughts

Training Maturity

It is unlikely that any two athletes in the same squad or team will have exactly the same pre-conditioning (and conditioning) needs. This divergence will rest on their training maturity and their specific playing/participatory/injury history. It will be up to the coach to devise individual pre-conditioning programmes. Training planning is covered in detail in part 8.

Gender

Gender differences must also be considered. There are significant biomechanical differences between men and women that could lead to injury if not taken into account. This is not prejudice but physiological/biomechanical fact.

For example, female athletes are at four to seven times greater risk of anterior cruciate ligament (ACL) injury than their male counterparts playing at similar levels in the same sports. This is because of gender differences in hip and lower limb alignment, which can lead to increased knee joint torsion in women.

By providing a focused analysis, coach/athlete will readily appreciate how sports science can help the coach pre-condition against and evaluate the potential for injury.

What is the ACL?

The ACL is one of four ligaments that are critical to the stability of the knee joint. A ligament is made of tough fibrous material and functions to control excessive motion by limiting joint mobility. Without ligaments to control the knee, the joint would be unstable and prone to dislocation. The ACL prevents the tibia (shinbone) from sliding too far forwards and contributes stability to other movements at the joint, including angulation and rotation. When an ACL injury occurs the knee becomes less stable. The ACL injury is a problem because this instability can make sudden, pivoting movements difficult and make the knee more prone to developing osteoarthritis and cartilage tears. Surgery is usually required.

ACL injuries are particularly prevalent in field sports involving twisting and turning movements, such as football. Researchers from Norway performed a retrospective study of 176 footballing patients who had sustained serious knee injuries. They found that the overall incidence rate of injuries was 0.063 per 1000 game hours. Women sustained 0.10 injuries per 1000 game hours whereas men sustained only 0.057 injuries per 1000 game hours. (Reference: *Am. J. Sports Med.*, 1997, May-Jun; 25(3):341–5)

Age

Age obviously has a crucial effect on the likelihood of an athlete sustaining an injury. As indicated in part 1, there are numerous factors that need to be accounted for when designing a training programme for both younger and master athletes. However, pre-conditioning is vital, whatever the athlete's age.

Figure 2.3 Straight-leg Jump

Performing exercises such as the straight-leg jump can pre-condition against injury in all sports involving running

How to Pre-condition against ACL Injury (for Men and Women)

- Strengthen the knee joint with exercises such as leg extensions.
- Perform sideways and backward jumping movements, gradually increasing the number of repetitions and power component over numerous progressive workouts.
- Strengthen the muscles at the back of the thighs (the hamstrings). These muscles are generally weaker in females than males, and are important for stabilising the knee.

Reducing Injury through Lower Limb Strengthening

The following research indicates just how successful a pre-conditioning programme can be. It focused specifically on lower limb injury prevention in handball players.

Researchers from Norway looked at how ankle (and knee) injuries could be reduced in Norwegian teenage handball players during the 2002–03 season. The survey involved 1837 players, split into an intervention group (958 players) and a control group (879 players). The former performed exercises designed to improve awareness and control of the ankles and knees during standing, running, cutting, jumping and landing. The exercises included those with a ball and the use of wobble boards. They covered warm-up, sport technique, balance and strength. Players spent four to five minutes on each group of exercises for a total of 15 to 20 minutes for the first 15 training sessions, and thereafter once per week. Coaches recorded attendance and details of the sessions. The control group continued with their normal training methods. So what did the team discover?

During the season, 262 players (14 per cent) were injured at least once (241 acute and 57 overuse injuries). Of these, the intervention group had lower risks than the control group when it came to sustaining acute knee or ankle injuries. Rate ratios for moderate and major injuries (defined as absence from play for 8 to 21 days) were also lower for the intervention group for all injuries. Risk of injury did not differ between young men and women.

The researchers concluded that, 'The rate of acute knee and ankle injuries and all injuries to young handball players was reduced by half by a structured program designed to improve knee and ankle control during play.' (Reference: *Med. Sci. Sports Exerc.*, 1981; 13(5):325–8)

X-Training as a Form of Pre-conditioning

The term X-Training is used to describe exercises that have little obvious relevance to an athlete's sport. A rugby player using an indoor rowing machine for training is a good example. X-Training can play a role in pre-conditioning and reducing injury, although it will be unlikely to improve – in the example given – specific rugby playing ability.

If properly tailored, X-Training workouts for sport can:

- enhance/maintain energy pathway fitness;
- aid recovery;
- provide fresh mental stimulation.

Cycling as X-Training for Runners

Researchers set about discovering whether substituting 50 per cent of run training volume with cycling would maintain 3000m track race performance and VO2max during a five-week recuperative phase at the end of the cross-country season. Eleven college runners were assigned to:

- a run-only training group;
- a cycle and run training group, which performed the different activities on different days.

Both groups trained at 75–80 per cent of maximum heart rate. Training volumes were similar to the competitive season, except that cycling made up 50 per cent of the volume for the cycle and run group.

So what did the team discover? The 3000m race time was 1.4 per cent (nine seconds) slower in the run training group and only 3.4 per cent (22 seconds) slower in the running and cycling group.

Equally important was the discovery that no significant change was found in VO2 max between either group. (Reference: *J. Strength Cond. Res.* 2003 May; 17(2):319–23)

The implication of these research findings for coaches is that cycling for endurance runners may enable the athlete's body greater time to recover from tough training/competitive training phases and improve future injury resilience.

The run and cycle group were only marginally slower. In terms of maintaining fitness in a year-long training plan, this could be seen as positive, especially when one considers that overuse injuries are a great possibility if running alone is performed. Successful conditioning is founded on developing fitness over a year or more; sometimes an athlete will have to lose some performance potential at one stage in the training year in order to improve it at another. Hence the decrease in 3000m run time identified in the study would not be regarded as significant in the greater scheme of things and could actually be beneficial.

PART **THREE**

WARMING UP FOR SPORT

For years, athletes in the majority of sports would warm up – prepare for their sport – by raising their body temperature with 5 to 15 minutes of gentle cardiovascular exercise, such as jogging, usually followed by static stretching movements. As a long-jump athlete, I was brought up on this 'traditional' warm-up format. I'd jog a couple of laps, get really warm, then sit and chat for the next half hour while supposedly stretching! When it came to doing the specific part of my workout, I'd often be cold, physically and mentally. My body and mind would have literally switched off, leaving me unprepared for the dynamic activity to follow. There are much more effective ways to warm up for all sports.

Note: Many of the exercises referenced in the previous pre-conditioning part are suitable for inclusion in the sport-specific warm-up, such as leg cycling.

The Sport-specific Warm-up

The sport-specific warm-up originated in the former Soviet bloc, particularly for speed and power athletes. From the 1970s or earlier, their athletes were using these types of warm-up, but it is only recently that they have become popular in The West. The sport-specific warm-up is designed to prepare the body and mind optimally for sport. It is relatively short, focused and progressively dynamic.

Virtually regardless of sport, the sport-specific warm-up should:

- be progressively dynamic, with exercises progressing to 'real' sport speed;
- include exercises that mimic the movements required in the relevant sport;
- raise body temperature – this process will 'switch on' numerous physiological processes that make subsequent vigorous exercise more effective and safer;
- fire up the neuromuscular system to unleash physiologically heightened performance;
- put the athlete in the right frame of mind to get the best from their body (known to sports psychologists as being in the 'zone of optimal functioning' or simply 'in the zone');
- improve sport-specific range of movement (SSROM) due to decreases in viscous resistance (muscles become literally more stretchy);
- increase oxygen utilisation in muscles, as

haemoglobin* release is facilitated at higher body temperatures.

Sports Training Tip

Exercise physiologists have often challenged the physical value of a warm-up. However, for an athlete to enter a competitive or training situation without prior preparation seems inconceivable. The rationale behind the sports-specific warm-up is at least much stronger than the older, traditional warm-up format.

The Sport-specific Warm-up Can Reduce Injury

Recent research (see below) has identified a reduced risk of injury when performing progressively quicker and, crucially, sport-specific stretches/movements. The psychological value of the warm-up cannot be negated either as a means of switching the athlete's mind on to their performance.

Specific Sport Focus – Warming up for Football

Professor Angel Spassov is a Bulgarian conditioning expert based in the United States. A football specialist, he has worked with six World Cup squads, and most recently with Portugal's Euro 2002 squad. He has designed a thorough and specific way to warm up for football (although the model can be applied, with minor adaptations, to most speed and endurance sports).

Spassov's warm-up involves both passive and active elements. For the passive part, he advises players to loosen their muscles 30 to 60 minutes before the game by rubbing their ankles, knees,

---

* Haemoglobin is the major element of red blood cells. It is an iron/protein compound that boosts the oxygen-carrying ability of blood about 65 times.

leg muscles, lower back, neck and shoulders with a heating ointment, preferably one that is odourless and not too hot on the skin.

The active warm-up that follows is divided into two parts:

1 **General.** This begins with six to eight minutes of jogging, followed by neck, shoulder, lower back and abdominal stretches. There should be two or three different routines, with 10 to 12 repetitions of each. Next, legs (hamstrings, hip flexors, abductors, adductors, quads and calf muscle) are targeted with passive and dynamic stretches (two to three standard routines with 10 to 12 repetitions and performance speed increased every set for the dynamic stretches). Next, varying-intensity sprints are performed in different directions. At the end of this part of the warm-up, players' pulse rates should have reached 160–170 beats per minute.

2 **Specific.** This begins with various kicks of the ball with both legs and various technical moves with the ball, such as dribbling and stopping the ball. These should progress to medium intensity and be performed with another player, then to high intensity with players combining into groups to practise all the technical skills at the highest possible intensity and speed.

Spassov's suggested warm-up makes great sense and should control players' progression to match readiness. With the early parts of the warm-up performed individually, players should be able to focus on their own movements and progression and not be tempted to perform movements that are too dynamic before their muscles are fully prepared. For more information on Spassov go to www.over-speedtraining.com

Dynamic stretches include leg cycling and lunges; descriptions follow.

Sports Training Tip

The coach/manager can play a vital warm-up role:

- They can direct and control the warm-up.
- They can brief their athletes on appropriate strategy and kit.
- They can boost or reduce the athletes' levels of arousal (see part 9).

Sports Training Tip

Potentiation may offer speed and power athletes a legal competitive boost and could be included as part of their warm-up. Potentiation primes fast twitch muscle fibre, increasing its level of power release. This is achieved by performing related plyometric or weight-training exercises (that work the same muscle groups) prior to performing a related sports skill, such as a sprint. For example, an athlete could perform four single-leg squats at 75 per cent of 1 repetition maximum before performing a 20m sprint. Research indicates that in this case sprint performance will be enhanced (see page 109 for more detail).

Static Stretches

When employed in the sport-specific warm-up, static stretches should be performed only as a peripheral element. They could be used, for example, to elongate muscles that are prone to tightness during endurance exercise. Using rowing as an example, rowers could concentrate on stretching the lower back and forearms to reduce potential tension build-up in these areas.

Static stretching methods are covered in detail on pages 47–8.

Don't Wear Shoes!

I am not recommending that you complete your next football session in your socks! However, if weather permits or you are training indoors or on a dry athletics track, then performing some of the sport-specific warm-up drills described on pages 41–6 over 10–20m without shoes can be very beneficial (a technique used by Olympic gold medal sprinter Jason Gardener, among others).

Because of their thick mid-soles, normal running shoes prevent the calf muscles and Achilles tendons from flexing optimally. They also reduce the athlete's ability to specifically strengthen these areas and the foot itself (research has shown that stronger feet can enhance speed and agility). Barefoot training should be progressed gradually, as years of wearing sports shoes for training will have reduced the resilience of the feet and lower limbs.

It is interesting to note that Nike have recently designed a shoe to mimic the action of the unshod foot – although it does beg the question of why you need a shoe to run in if the intention is to be barefoot!

Sports Training Tip

Athletes and coaches should make sure that their warm-up incorporates exercises that replicate specific elements of their sport. Examples include 'ghost' shots for a racket sports player and simulated kicks without a ball for rugby and football players. These drills should form part of the warm-up for all workouts, including weights and circuits as well as sport-specific practice and competition.

Sport-specific Warm-up Exercises

The exercises described in the following pages are applicable to the majority of sports. They should be performed after the athlete has raised their body temperature with a minimum of five minutes' jogging. Suggested repetitions are for example purposes only. Coach/athlete should consider their specific requirements.

Exercise 3.1   Lunge Walk

Great for: loosening the hips and hamstrings and strengthening the buttock and hamstring muscles

Take a large step forward into a lunge, then step forwards into another lunge. Keep the chest up and look straight ahead, coordinating arm and leg movements – opposite arm to leg. *Do 4 x 20m.*

Exercise 3.2   High Knee Lift

Great for: hip flexor and ankle strength

In an alternate stepping action, extend up on to the toes of one leg, while lifting the thigh of the other leg to a position parallel with the ground. Next, lower this leg and place the foot flat on the ground, before lifting the other thigh and extending from the ankle as before. Coordinate arms with legs and keep the chest elevated when moving forwards. The speed of the drill can be increased as the warm-up progresses. *Do 4 x 15m.*

Exercise 3.3	Elbow to Inside of Ankle Lunge

Exercise 3.4	Calf Walk

Great for: lower limb and Achilles tendon strength

Keep legs relatively straight and use a heel-to-toe action as you move forwards taking short steps. Coordinate the arms with the legs and keep the chest elevated. *Do 4 x 20m.*

Great for: hip flexibility and hamstring strength

The forward lean also stretches the lower back. This exercise is very similar to the lunge walk, except the athlete extends their trunk forwards over their front leg after they have lunged. So, if the right leg is to the front, the athlete takes their right elbow down to the inside of their right ankle.

Sideways and Backward Skipping/running

Great for: lower limb and ankle strength, agility and flexibility

Performing these drills will pre-condition against common running injuries, such as shin splints, and strengthen the knee and ankle joints. The athlete should focus on being 'light' on their feet and generating movement from the balls of their feet.

- **Sideways running**. Assume a side-on position with feet just beyond shoulder-width apart. Bend the knees to attain a three-quarter squat position. Lift the arms up and out to the sides until they are parallel with the ground. Move to the left or the right by pushing off from the inside foot, landing lightly first on the outside foot, then the inside foot, before pushing off into the next side step from the inside foot.

Exercise 3.5a   Sideways Running

• **Backward running.** The coach/athlete should obviously ensure that there is nothing behind them. From an upright position with feet shoulder-width apart, push off from the ball of one foot to land lightly on the ball of the other. Continue to push backwards in the same fashion. Step (lift and push) the legs back as you move backwards. Coordinate arms with legs. Perform the exercise at about 50 per cent effort until familiarity is gained and then progress to faster speeds. For a variation, on pushing back into each step, lift the legs up, out and back further to literally run in reverse. This will open up stride length and further develop quadriceps and calf muscle strength.

Sports Training Tip

Backward running is used as a rehabilitation exercise for people with back and knee injuries, as it places less strain on these areas. It is therefore a great pre-conditioning exercise to include in the training plan.

Exercise 3.5b   Backward running

Perform these exercises over 20m, taking a walk back recovery. *Do 3–4 repetitions.*

Exercise 3.6	Simulated Running Arm Action

Great for: preparing the shoulders and back for running

Assume a lunge position. Looking straight ahead, pump the arms backwards and forwards as if running, maintaining a 90-degree angle at the elbows throughout the drill. Try to remain as relaxed as possible. Pay attention to keeping the shoulders down and not 'wearing' them around the ears.

As a variation, this exercise can be performed from a seated position. This will develop greater core (back and stomach) stability, as the athlete will have to work harder through this area. Light dumbbells can be used to develop greater strength and speed, but their weight should not affect technique.

Perform either or both exercises for 15–60 seconds, alternating arm speed. *Do 2–4 sets.*

Exercise 3.7	Leg Drives

Great for: sharpening the athlete's mind and body

Use a wall or barrier for balance. Look straight ahead and keep the body straight. Next, lift the right leg until the thigh is parallel to the ground. Working from the hip, 'drive' (push) the leg back down so that the forefoot contacts the ground. Immediately on contact, pull the leg back to the starting position. *Do 3 x 10 on each leg, gradually increasing the speed of the drive.*

Exercise 3.8 Leg Cycling

Great for: specifically warming up the hamstrings for dynamic activity and solidifying the mechanics of good sprinting form

Assume the same starting position as for the leg drives exercise (*see* above), but this time, after driving the leg down, sweep it behind you before pulling it through from the hip back up to the starting position. This exercise should be performed slowly at first before gradually building up speed as confidence is gained. *Do 20 repetitions on each leg, 2–4 sets.*

Exercise 3.9 'Walking' Running Action Drill

Great for: base strength for running

Stand with feet slightly apart. Lift the thigh of one leg to a position parallel to the ground, while at the same time pushing up on to the toes of the grounded foot. Claw forwards with the suspended leg and then let the foot come down to the ground, while lifting and pulling the previously grounded foot through to perform the next stride simultaneously. Try to bring the heel close to the buttock during the pull-through. In doing so the athlete is basically performing a slow-paced running action. The arms should be coordinated with the legs (opposite arm to leg). *Do 4 x 20m with a slow recovery walk back.*

Sports Training Tip

Many of the exercises involved in a sport-specific warm-up reduce risk of injury because they strengthen muscles, tendons and ligaments in a way that is highly relevant to the sport.

Warming up and Substitutes

Substitutes in team sports should regularly warm up along the touchline or other designated area in an attempt to maintain competitive readiness. They, like their playing counterparts, should remain hydrated (see part 10) during their time 'on the bench', as regular periods of warming up during the match can lead to dehydration and impaired performance.

Warm clothing should be used on cold days to preserve body temperature. Conversely, on hot days, it is recommended that substitutes (and those in the starting line-up when they warm up for the start of the match) do not allow their body temperature to increase above 22°C, as this can have a deleterious effect on performance (see 'Precooling', part 6). Note: This recommendation can apply to any athlete warming up on a hot day.

The Relevance of Static Stretching to Sport

Despite the crucial importance of the sport-specific warm-up and its relative lack of emphasis on static stretching, there is still a place for this type of stretching in an athlete's training plan.

Athletes and coaches will probably be familiar with static held (active/passive-type) stretches, such as bending down to the toes to stretch the hamstrings. Although these have little relevance to specifically preparing the body for dynamic sports activity, there is still a need to incorporate them and other similar styles of stretching into an athlete's training, for the following reasons:

- **To improve sport-specific range of movement (SSROM).** If a footballer has tight hamstrings, quadriceps and hip muscles, they may be more prone to muscle strain when kicking and running. Static stretching can help them attain and maintain SSROM.
- **To aid relaxation and recovery.** Because of the dynamic nature of most sports, training can tighten muscles. Regular passive stretching will combat this tightness and aid recovery.
- **To boost the effectiveness of the warm-down.** The athlete can also stretch for five to ten minutes as part of their post-training warm-down to aid recovery and elongate muscles that may have tightened during their workout.

Traditional Stretching Methods

I have provided descriptions of the main static stretching methods that athlete/coach could incorporate into their sports training plans. Note, though, that prolonged static stretching should be avoided in a sport-specific warm-up as it can have a detrimental effect on performance. There is also virtually no research that indicates that static stretching in a warm-up can reduce injury; on the contrary, recent research suggests that this type of stretching can actually increase muscle (hamstring) strain (see page 52, 'Beating Hamstring Injuries in Football').

Passive Stretching

A passive stretch is attained by easing into it without jerky or dynamic movements, with the end position held for 15–20 seconds. Gravity or external force (the latter provided by the athlete, a training partner, machine, belt or rope) supplies the means to stretch.

Figure 3.1 Lying Hamstring (Passive) Stretch

This type of stretch is more sport-specific than passive stretches because muscles are moved and held in place by their own actions, just as they are in sport.

Raising one arm up straight by the ear in alignment with the body and holding it there for 10–15 seconds is a typical example of an active stretch. Another is pulling one leg back as far as possible from the hip from a lying-on-the-back position: the leg being stretched can be folded at the knee or extended.

PNF Stretching

Proprioceptive neuromuscular facilitation (PNF) stretching is often recommended as one of the best ways to improve everyday range of movement (ROM) and sport-specific ROM. Although it is possible for an athlete to perform PNF stretches on their own, perhaps with the aid of a towel or a band, they will get more from them if they have a partner to assist them. PNF works on the basis of two-directional force increasing the stretch potential of the muscles by short-circuiting the stretch/reflex (*see* page 14).

Figure 3.2 PNF Stretch (Hamstring)

Active Stretching

Active stretching involves holding the stretch. Although this may sound the same as a passive stretch, there is actually a big difference as an active stretch utilises muscular strength to hold the stretched muscle in position.

PNF Stretch for the Hamstrings

The athlete should lie on their back on the floor with their arms by their sides. A training partner/coach should lift one leg up and back towards the athlete's head. They should maintain a slight bend at the knee joint of the active leg, with the other leg pressed flat against the ground. The leg being stretched will travel back to a point where further movement becomes difficult. This position should be held for 20 seconds. The athlete should then push back against the partner through their leg (the partner must obviously be braced and ready to offer resistance). Relax, then repeat for a further 15 seconds. At this point the athlete should find that their range of movement is increased.

The sticking point for a stretch is created by the stretch/reflex mechanism (see page 14).

'Sharpening' Drills in Warm-up

It is important that the athlete's warm-up switches on their neuromuscular system so that they are in the right state of physical and, crucially, mental readiness to participate in their sport activity.

A boxer or martial artist will need quick reactions when they enter the ring or step on to the dojo. If they (or, physiologically, their neuromuscular system) are not 'sharp' then they could be making a speedy exit. The same concept applies to other athletes, particularly speed and power athletes, who need to move their body as fast or as near to as fast as possible to produce winning sports performance.

A range of drills/exercises can be used to boost this readiness. Some of the drills that follow are, although not necessarily sport-specific in terms of their movement pattern,

Warm-up Stretching Slows Sprint Speed

Sports scientists studied the effect of 30-second passive stretches on the 20-metre sprint times of collegiate athletes. The hamstrings, quadriceps and calf muscles were all stretched – key muscle groups involved in sprinting. Sprint times were increased in all cases. (Reference: *Sports Sci.*, 2005; 23: 449–54)

Warm-up Stretching Impairs Strength

Researchers considered the impact of 15 seconds of passive hip, thigh and calf stretches to the one repetition maximum (1RM) leg extension and leg flexion performance of physical education students. It was discovered that the stretches reduced leg extension strength by 8.1 per cent and leg flexion by 7.3 per cent over 1RM attempts made without prior stretching. (Reference: *Res Q Exerc. Sport*, 1998; 69: 411–415)

For coaches, the implications of this research are that they should consider very carefully the value of passive-type stretching in warm-up. Select sport-specific (functional) movements that will warm the athlete up specifically for their sport activity.

specifically designed to make the athlete feel 'ready', 'combative' and able to effect quick movements. They may even increase levels of arousal (*see* pages 178–9, part 9).

Only a few repetitions (four to six) of these exercises should be performed prior to competitions or workouts where 'flat-out' or 'near-to' speeds are required. They should form part of the later stage of the sport-specific warm-up, when the body is 'ready' for dynamic and intense movement. Note: Many of the exercises described previously will serve a similar purpose if performed at maximum effort.

Exercise 3.10	Body Rotation from Short-stance Lunge Position

Exercise 3.11 Hand to Knee Drill

The athlete takes a medium step forwards into a lunge, keeping the chest elevated and looking straight ahead. They should aim to 'feel' light on their feet. When ready and as fast as possible, they should rotate their body through 180 degrees, so that they face the opposite way to which they started. The movement is initiated by twisting through the ankles, knees and hips; they should then pause before rotating back the other way.

Do twice in each direction.

The athlete assumes a similar lunge position as for the above exercise. They should hold the palm of one hand out just above parallel to the ground. When ready, or at the command of their coach/other player/training partner, they should drive the leg on the same side as the hand as quickly as they can, so that the knee contacts the palm of their hand. This should be done without taking the hand to the knee.

Do five times on each side and then change sides.

Exercise 3.12	Chest Pass of Football/ Medicine Ball against Wall

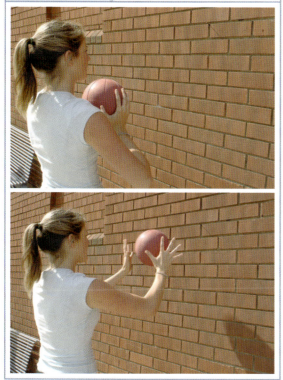

The athlete should stand approximately 1 metre from a wall. They then perform a series of chest passes against the wall as fast as they can. A football will require much quicker reactions than a 2–5kg medicine ball.

With thought and improvisation, coach and athlete can devise other similar drills, perhaps more relevant to their sport. As noted, these drills are designed to increase the athlete's neuromuscular sense of readiness. They may be useful for 'those days' when getting psyched up and in the zone is less easy. Obviously, these drills are suited to speed and high power sport activities. I do not recommend their use by golfers, for example, or other sports that require a much more controlled application of sport skill and aggression. Here, breathing techniques such as centring may be far more appropriate (*see* page 178).

Sports Training Tip

The sport-specific warm-up should include specific mental preparation (as should all conditioning). As I stress throughout this book, the physical aspect of training cannot be removed from the mental aspect if optimum sport performance is to ensue. Athletes should focus on the training session/ competition as a part of the sport-specific warm-up. Five minutes could be set aside to do this prior to the physical warm-up.

Sports Training Tip

It is necessary to get 'into the zone' to optimally recruit fast twitch muscle fibre, particularly type IIb fibre. However, this must not be achieved at the expense of smooth technique. Trying too hard can reduce the effective application of sport technique. Stretching and breathing exercises can relax an athlete before their competition, but this must not become a preoccupation as dynamic performance can be impaired.

Beating Hamstring Injuries in Football

It is beyond the scope of this book to specifically address football conditioning and pre-conditioning methods (readers interested in a full appraisal of this subject should consult S. Thadani, *Soccer Conditioning*, A&C Black, 2006. However, I do want to focus on hamstring protection, as hamstring injuries are common in football and other sports.

Researchers investigated the relationship between current flexibility training protocols and hamstring strain rates (HSRs) in English professional football clubs. Data on flexibility training was collected from 30 clubs in the four divisions during the 1998/99 season.

Although there was considerable variation in the way the different clubs trained for flexibility, the researchers discovered that static (passive) stretching was the most popular method used (surprising, given its limited relevance to match and training conditions, as noted previously).

In terms of injuries, hamstring strains accounted for 11 per cent of the total and a third of all muscle strains, while about 14 per cent of hamstring strains were re-injuries. HSRs were most prevalent in the Premiership (13.3 for every 1000 playing hours) and least prevalent in Division 2 (7.8 per 1000 hours), with forwards most likely to be injured. Most (97 per cent) hamstring strains were grade one and two (hamstring trains are graded one, two or three, depending on severity – a grade one might consist of small micro-tears in the muscle; a grade two would be a partial tear in the muscle and grade three is a severe or complete rupture of the muscle). Two-thirds of strains occurred late during training/matches. Football coaches, and other similar field sport coaches, should therefore consider this factor and look at the specific conditioning of endurance for their players.

When analysing injury rates in relation to flexibility protocols, the researchers correlated that about 80 per cent of HSR variability was accounted for by stretching holding time. Statistically, the length of time a muscle was stretched was the single highest predictor when accounting for 30 per cent of hamstring injuries. (Reference: *Br. J. Sports Med.*, 2004 Dec; 38(6):793)

If hamstring strains are to be reduced, in this case among elite football players, club coaches and players need to be better educated on the merits of active (sport-specific) warm-ups, including specific stretches (see *also* page 26 for the importance of eccentric muscular action conditioning as a means to reduce hamstring and other soft tissue injury).

PART **FOUR**

DEVELOPING STRENGTH

Virtually no sports performer neglects weight-training. At the Manchester Commonwealth Games in 2002, even England's lawn bowling team weight-trained to improve their performance. Performing the 'right' strength and weight-training in a sports conditioning programme is vital for enhanced performance. The right training programme could put the athlete on the medal rostrum, while the wrong one could leave them at the back of the field.

This part also focuses on and references other 'resistance' training options, such as circuit training methods, and the use of more specialist strength-training equipment, such as Kettlebells and Fit-balls, for sports conditioning.

It should be read in conjunction with part 5, Developing Power, if coach and athlete are to fully understand, develop and implement the most effective, usable and relevant 'strength' for their sport.

Getting the Most from Weight-training

Over the years I have seen many track and field athletes place too much emphasis on their weight-training. They build prodigious amounts of strength throughout the winter/preparatory training months, then come out to perform in the spring/competitive season full of expectation. However, their expectation may soon be shattered, as although they are undoubtedly stronger, they are not any faster or more agile. This often results in no performance gains and, on occasions, even worse performance than in previous seasons. From a conditioning perspective, there are a number of reasons for this:

- The athlete may have gained weight because muscle weighs significantly more than other body tissue. This means that their 'power-to-weight ratio' (see below) will have decreased. (Note: Certain types of weight-training methods are more likely to increase body weight because of their hormonal response, see page 91).
- Athlete/coach may not have 'channelled' the strength gained in the gym effectively into sport-specific requirements. This is all the more likely if they have not followed a systematic training plan.
- Athlete/coach may not be aware of the limited direct relevance of weight-training to specifically enhancing sports performance.
- Athlete/coach may not have selected the 'right' weight-training exercises for their sport.

All of these considerations are examined more closely later in the part.

Power-to-weight Ratio

As muscle has denser properties than other body tissue, it is crucial to balance muscular gain against ideal performance weight. Even if sports-enhancing strength gains are achieved through weight-training, it is possible that these could be cancelled out by increased body weight.

Jonathan Edwards, Olympic and World triple jump champion, had a superb power-to-weight ratio. He was extremely light (at his peak he weighed 65kg), yet was incredibly powerful, as he demonstrated in his best legal jump of 18.29m.

'Channelling' Weights Strength and the Specificity of Exercises

Coach and athlete should never lose sight of why they are training. If a weight-training programme is to be successful, the strength gained in the weights room must be channelled into *improved* sports performance. The channelling process takes the improved strength gained through lifting weights (or performing other resistance exercises), which in itself will not improve sports performance, through a process of increasingly more specific exercises (weights, body weight, sport drills and plyometrics). This should provide every opportunity for sports performance to be positively affected.

Everything else being equal, a larger, stronger, weight-trained muscle will be able to produce greater power and/or be more fatigue-resistant than a non-weight-trained one.

In table 4.1 (*see* page 76) you will see how strength can be progressed from general weight-training exercise through to a more specific weight or other exercise. This will make the strength gains more likely to boost the athlete's performance.

Pages 62–74 provide a detailed consideration of selected weight-training exercises, identifying their relevance to various sports.

Weight-training Exercises

- **General:** These condition the muscles used in a sporting movement in a broadly similar way to the movement involved in the sport itself. For example, the double leg squat will strengthen the upper thighs in a way that relates to running.
- **Specific:** A specific weight-training exercise provides a stronger correlation between the way it works muscles, speed of movement and actual sport performance. The single-leg squat, for example, provides a closer match to running activities than the double leg squat. This is because it is performed from one leg, as is running.

Speed of Movement

It takes around 0.5 seconds to perform a weight-training exercise, when it is performed as quickly as possible. This is appreciably slower than the execution of the majority of sport skills. As an example, an elite sprinter's foot may be in contact with the ground for less than 0.1 seconds. It is crucial that coach and athlete appreciate this. Although weight-training is an important option, its emphasis could be detrimental to sports performance unless it forms part of a carefully constructed training programme that specifically channels strength gained into sports performance.

Plyometric exercises (*see* part 5) offer much greater 'matched' sport power and speed of movement possibilities.

Specialist Weight-training Exercises for Developing Rotational Sports Strength and Speed

Researchers looked at the forces generated in a baseball hit and found that the batter's hip segment rotates to a maximum speed of 714 degrees per second, followed by a shoulder segment rotation of up to 937 degrees per second. The product of this kinetic link is a maximum linear bat velocity of 31 metres per second. (Reference: *J. Orthop. Sports Phys. Therapy*, 1995 Nov; 22(5): 193–201) The golf swing, to give another example, can be completed in a mere 250 milliseconds.[7]

It would be virtually impossible to develop the 'wind-up and rotate' velocities required for these and other sports through weight-training alone. However, developing a base for this type of speed is possible through weight-training and carefully constructed channelling exercises.

To reiterate, coach/athlete should note that weight-training can provide a foundation for improving sport-specific power and endurance, but in itself is very unlikely to improve performance. There are far more specialist, specific and effective ways of improving sports performance.

Weight-training Fast Twitch Muscle Fibre for Speed and Power

As explained in part 1, the way fast twitch muscle fibre is trained is crucial for the development of speed and power.

Type IIb fast twitch fibre is crucial for the out-and-out power/speed athlete, such as a sprinter, while type IIa fibre offers a reduced but potentially powerful output. This fibre type would be developed by field sport players as well as out-and-out power/speed athletes. The ability of both fibre types to contract quickly and forcibly can be enhanced by weight-training and other resistance methods.

However, because of the amount of neural (mental) stimulation required to activate type IIb fibre, it is argued that weight-training may recruit only relatively small amounts of it, and actually primarily targets type IIa fibre. Indeed, it is further argued that type IIb fibre can be converted into type IIa by prolonged weight-training. This means that for those in search of out-and-out speed, a weight-training programme could actually slow them down. To avoid this undesirable outcome, coach/athlete should:

- use power combination training (*see* pages 105–8) and plyometric training as perhaps the key ingredients in speed and power development;
- reduce the quantity and intensity of weight-training as the competitive season approaches (*see* part 8).

Repetition Maximum (1RM) refers to the maximum amount of weight the athlete could lift once, on one exercise, such as the bench press. Knowing a real or estimated 1RM is very useful for developing different types of strength and systematically progressing training.

Weight-training Systems

It is beyond the scope of this book to provide a detailed consideration of all the weight-training systems than could be used to develop sports strength – there are literally hundreds. Readers with an interest in this subject should consult A. Bean, *The Complete Guide to Strength Training*, 3rd edition, A&C Black, 2005.

However, I have provided a basic overview of how combining different numbers of repetitions with different loading (weight on machine, weight on the bar and so on) as a percentage of 1RM with different speeds of the lifting movement can develop different types of strength.

Sports Training Tip

Rest between sets and the speed of lifting can affect the hormonal response to a weight-training session, and with it muscle mass, body weight and sports performance.

Developing Different Types of Strength

There are three broad types of sports strength that can be developed through weight-training – maximum strength, power strength and strength endurance. Each is determined by the percentage of 1RM that the athlete works at and the number of repetitions involved.

Figure 4.1 Strength Training (Weights)

Amount of weight lifted will have a significant effect on type of sports strength developed

Maximum Strength Weight-training

Targets: Fast twitch muscle fibre and has a medium to large effect on increasing muscle size

Sports relevance: All, but particularly speed- and power-based activities

Repetitions: 1–6

Weight lifted: 'Heavy' – 85 per cent plus of 1RM

Sets: 1–8

Recovery: 'Full' two to five minutes, to maintain quality and intensity. Training different body parts during different workouts can allow for greater recovery and strength adaptation, where applicable. At most, three maximum-strength workouts should be completed per week, with at least 24–36 hours' recovery between them.

Comment: Training for maximum strength is draining. If overload and adaptation are to be achieved, repetitions should be completed under conditions of 'strain', as for all weight-training systems. However, this should not be at the expense of good lifting technique. Mental focus is required to get the most from these workouts and to recruit the largest, most powerful fast twitch fibres.

Sports training tip: Athletes should work out with a training partner/coach when maximum strength weight-training and eccentric weight-training with heavy loads. It is the partner or coach's job to 'spot' – assist the athlete to return the bar to its starting position – if they cannot fully complete their repetitions. Their presence and words of encouragement will also motivate. It is crucial that a point of failure or near failure is reached if strength gains are to be made (this is sometimes referred to as the point of 'strain'; having a partner on hand will encourage this to be achieved).

Maximum strength weight-training suggested workouts:

a) 4 x 4 @ 85% 1RM
b) 3 x 2 @ 90% 1RM
c) 8 x 1 @ 95% 1RM

Number of exercises: 4–6. Select exercises that are broadly applicable to the sport being trained for.

Power Weight-training

Targets: Fast twitch muscle fibre and has a potentially major effect on increasing muscle size, due to hormonal response

Sports relevance: All, including endurance sports

Repetitions: 4–10

Weight lifted: 'Medium/heavy', that is 65–85 per cent of 1RM

Sets: 2–6

Recovery: See Table 4.2 with its comments on the hormonal response to this type of workout

Comment: Power weight-training is as intense as maximum strength weight-training, if not more so. It requires dynamic but *controlled* lifting. The athlete attempts to move the weight as fast as possible but without compromising good technique. Positive mental focus is required to maximise the outcomes of these workouts; the athlete will achieve very little if they are not 'in the zone' (for exercises that may assist the athlete prepare mentally and physically for this type of workout, *see* 'Hand to Knee Drill', page 50).

Power weight-training suggested workouts:

a) 3 x 8 @ 70% 1RM
b) 4 x 4 @ 80% 1RM

Number of exercises: 4–6. Select major muscle group exercises that have a relationship to the sport being trained for.

Strength Endurance Weight-training

Strength endurance weight-training is basically a form of circuit training (specifically, circuit resistance training, *see* page 77).

Targets: Slow twitch muscle fibre and fast twitch type IIa, and has little effect on increasing muscle size

Sports relevance: All

Repetitions: 10–20 plus (or performed within a given timeframe, such as 30 seconds)

Weight lifted: 'Light/medium', that is 45–65 per cent @ 1RM

Sets: 4–8 plus

Recovery: This should be kept to a minimum as the aim is to develop the muscles' ability to sustain repeated contractions under conditions of increasing fatigue

Comment: Strength endurance weight-training deliberately overloads the body to achieve a fatigued state. The athlete may be unable to complete the designated number of repetitions in a set. Lifting technique will probably suffer as a consequence, so both coach and athlete should be mindful of the potential injury risk. It is therefore better to stop performing a set of exercises when chronic fatigue takes over (or to reduce the weight lifted), rather than attempting to continue and risk injury.

Strength endurance weight-training suggested workouts

5 x 20 @ 45% 1RM

Number of Exercises: 6–15. For a specific example of strength endurance weight-training for rowing, *see* page 79.

Back Safety and Neutral Spine Position

The chances of back injury occurring can be increased when weight-training. However, this can be minimised if the athlete performs each exercise as technically correctly as possible (even under conditions of fatigue) and, where applicable, maintains neutral spine position.

Neutral spine position optimally distributes force through the back. It results in a posture that is neither bowed nor hyper-extended (bent backwards).

How to Achieve Neutral Spine Position

Figure 4.2 Neutral Spine Position

The athlete should stand with their heels touching or nearly touching a wall and lightly press their buttocks and shoulders against it. This posture should be kept in mind and adhered to when weight-lifting and, where achievable, when performing other sports skills and drills.

Neutral Pelvis/Hip Position

Achieving a neutral pelvis position can also reduce potential back strain. It distributes some of the loading forces the back is subject to on to the buttock muscles. This creates greater structural integrity across the body.

It is more difficult to describe how to achieve the required pelvic position (being familiar with pelvic floor exercises will be an advantage here). Basically, neutral pelvis position is attained by tilting/rotating the pelvis, usually forwards (the pelvis should be able to move through an arc of 6–7cm when isolated and rocked backwards and forwards). The neutral position will be dependent on the performer's existing pelvic mobility. As a guide, the right position will be achieved when the back is in neutral position and the chest more elevated. Correct positioning will probably make the athlete feel taller.

Athletes should try to hold both neutral pelvis and spine position throughout their training and competition, where specific sports and exercise requirements permit.

Fixed or Free Weights?

Research backs up the assumptions of most coaches/athletes that free-weight exercises (as opposed to fixed/machine weights) are best for developing sport-specific strength.

Research teams in Scotland and America found that free weights were superior to fixed-weight installations due to their ability to permit:

- a more closely related speed of movement;
- greater movement pattern specificity;
- greater joint angle specificity (machines can restrict strength curves to limited ranges);
- multi-joint exercises

and to involve numerous stabilising and balance-assisting muscles. (Reference: *Strength and Conditioning Journal*, vol. 22; no 3: pp. 65–66)

Athletes should therefore be encouraged to use free weights. However, they must become technically proficient before lifting powerfully and heavily and when deliberately and significantly overloading the body.

Sports Training Tip

Failure to align strength gains with sports technique will invariably result in impaired performance. This led Soviet sports scientists and coaches to develop the skill/strength periodisation (SSP) model of training planning. This method aims to match strength (and speed) with skill acquisition and technical performance. SSP and other periodisation models are covered in detail in part 8.

Sports Training Tip

Combining weight-training and plyometric exercises to create a 'power combination' workout is highly effective, building power and targeting fast twitch muscle fibres (see page 85).

The Effects of Detraining on Fast Twitch Muscle Fibre

Research has shown that if an athlete does not weight-train for a period of weeks, their number of type IIb muscle fibres can increase. This will prepare them for powerful, short-lived sport activity, such as sprinting, and is an important consideration when planning a peak for such athletes. It should be noted that this alteration in fast twitch muscle fibre assumes that the athlete has previously been participating in a relevant and prolonged weight-training programme. (References: *Sports Med.*, 2001; 31(15): 106–82 and *Acta Physiologica Scandanavica*; 151: 135–142)

The coach therefore needs to consider the periodisation of weight-training programmes to develop peak performance. They also have to balance this against the consideration that too long a lay-off from weights can negatively affect performance, as base levels of strength are lost. Also, in sports where muscle size and mass is important, such as the shot put and for American football line-men, too long a lay-off from weights can impair the athletes' performance effectiveness. Consequently, the coach must always be looking to maintain a predetermined base of strength/power and muscle mass from which the athlete can optimally perform.

Selected Sport-specific Weight-training Exercises

Coach/athlete should study the detailed exercise descriptions provided on pages 62–74 to increase their understanding of how to develop sport-specific strength through weight-training. Take particular note of the exercise progressions to identify how the strength gained through a weight-training exercise can be channelled into more specific resistance exercises, giving every opportunity for improved sports performance. These 'progression' exercises increasingly match the actual playing and competition demands of sport. Many of these take the form of dynamic movement plyometric exercises (*see* part 5). Descriptions of further exercises and sport-specific progressions are provided in Table 4.1 (*see* page 75).

Where provided, suggested repetitions and sets are for guideline purposes only.

Exercise 4.1	Supine Dumbbell Straight-arm Pullover

'Triangular' Grip

Muscles involved: Sides of upper back (latissimus dorsi); backs of shoulders (posterior deltoids); backs of upper arms (triceps)
Sports applicability: Sports involving an

overhead hitting/throwing motion, such as tennis, the javelin and the football throw-in

Conditioning benefits:

- *General:* This exercise can be performed by athletes with varying degrees of strength, although it becomes more of an advanced exercise when heavy weights or a dynamic throwing action are used. In this guise it should only be performed by the well-conditioned.
- *Sport-specific:* The exercise has a great pre-conditioning value, as it can strengthen soft tissue for much more dynamic sports-related activity, thus reducing injury potential.

Start position:

1 Lie supine on a bench and place the feet on the floor or, depending on leg length, a step or similar platform. Ensure that a) the back remains in neutral alignment on the bench and b) a stable position is achieved.
2 Hold a fixed-weight, non-adjustable dumbbell over the chest with both hands, using a 'triangular' grip. The palms should be held up with the fingers pointing away from the head.
3 Maintain a slight bend at the elbows and rotate the shoulders inwards slightly.

Action:

4 Take the dumbbell back and behind the head by lowering the arms. Do not allow the elbows to move outside the line of the body.
5 Change from lowering to lifting the dumbbell when the upper arms are approximately 20–30 degrees above parallel to the floor.

Training tips:

- Avoid hyper-extending the wrists. Keep them in a neutral position while performing the exercise.
- Brace the abdominal and back muscles when

lowering the dumbbell behind the head to avoid hyper-extending the back.

Sport-specific Exercise Progressions

Fit-ball supine straight-arm pullover: A similar starting position is used as for the bench version, with the upper back supported on the Fit-ball and the feet firmly planted on the floor. While performing the straight-arm pullover, the inherent instability of the ball will require greater active stabilisation throughout the core. This will mean that a) more muscle fibre is recruited from this region and b) the exercise is made more sport-specific because the core *works* to transfer and optimise the power expressed by the arms, as it does in most sports situations.

Fit-ball supine medicine ball throw: This exercise can be viewed as being at the top of the conditioning chain for those athletes involved in dynamic throwing and hitting sports, in terms of the progression of exercises so far provided. From the same starting position as the previous exercise, hold a light medicine ball in two hands at arms' length over the chest. Take the arms back (either straight or bent) then bring them forwards dynamically to throw the ball to a partner or against a wall. Power should be generated through the core before being released through the arms.

Exercise 4.2	Fit-ball Supine Medicine Ball Throw	Exercise 4.3	Standing Machine Calf Raise

Muscles involved: Gastrocnemius, soleus (calf muscles)

Sports applicability: All sports, particularly those involving running and jumping

Conditioning benefits:

- *General:* The standing machine calf raise is a great exercise for targeting the lower leg muscles due to the fact that a straight leg position is maintained throughout. The prime mover is the gastrocnemius, as this muscle is best suited to developing force from this stretched position. Note: seated calf raise exercises emphasis the soleus muscle.

- *Sport-specific:* Many athletes neglect the calf muscles in their sports conditioning programmes in favour of exercises, such as the squat and leg press, that emphasise the larger thigh muscles. However, a failure to condition the smaller calf muscles appropriately will reduce the ability of the athlete to develop optimum propulsive power for running- and agility-based sports. The lower legs (ankle and foot) are crucial in this respect, as the more effective these areas are at cushioning and returning force, the quicker and more dynamic the athlete will be. Additionally, as mentioned in part 2, research indicates that heavy weight machine (or free-weight) eccentric standing calf raises are very effective at conditioning out potential Achilles tendon problems.

Start position:

1 Stand tall under the machine's pads and take hold of the grips with elbows flexed. The feet should be facing forwards, not splayed out or in.
2 Look straight ahead and keep the back in neutral alignment.

3 Keep the ankles, knees and hips in alignment.
4 Make sure the ankles are lined up with one another on the machine's footplate and that the toes support the athlete's weight.
5 The standing calf raise machine allows the exercise to be performed with the heels positioned below the toes – this works the calf muscles over a greater range of movement. However, this facility should not be forced, to avoid excess strain being placed on either the calf muscles or the Achilles tendons.

Action:

6 Contract the calf muscles to lift the body.
7 Lift to full ankle extension, pause and lower (the eccentric muscular contraction) under control. Because of the exercise's remedial/injury-prevention capability, do so to a count of three to four seconds.

Training tips: The athlete should look straight ahead and focus their balance so that it is evenly distributed across the toes. This will avoid rolling the ankles over or inwards, which could lead to injury.

Variations and Sport-specific Exercise
Progression

Single-leg body weight calf raise: Calf raise
exercises can be made more sport-specific by
performing them from a free-standing position
– with or without the use of weights. These
exercises develop 'kinesthetic'* ability and
recruit numerous, much smaller stabilising
muscles that are often not significantly challenged by fixed-weight machines. To perform
the exercise, stand on one leg, with the other
tucked up towards the buttocks, and the arms
positioned by the sides to aid balance. Extend
up on to the toes and lower slowly. Begin with
3 x 10 single-leg calf raises on each leg, taking
90 seconds' recovery between sets. Once the
athlete can handle these comfortably, the
difficulty can be increased by holding light
dumbbells (10kg) in each hand.

Straight-leg jumps: This progression develops
dynamic lower-leg power. From a standing
position, use the feet, ankles and calf muscles
to propel the body into the air. Land 'light', but
react as quickly as possible to the ground. Use
the arms to assist the jump by swinging them
back and up in time with the jump.

Exercise 4.4   Straight-leg Jumps

---

* Kinesthesis refers to awareness of body in space and movement and the skills necessary to maintain this awareness and
control the body to perform technical and physical movements.

Split Squat

Muscles involved: Quadriceps, hamstrings, gluteus maximus

Sports applicability: All sports; particularly relevant to running

Conditioning benefits:

- *General*: The split squat is basically a single-leg squat. It is an exercise that can be performed by athletes with varying degrees of strength, although it becomes more of an advanced exercise when heavy weights are used. In this guise it should be performed only by the well-conditioned.
- *Sport-specific*: The exercise offers a great deal to the athlete looking for greater sport-specific leg strength and power. This reflects the fact that the split squat works one leg at a time and requires a degree of balance to perform – both key aspects of sports performance.

Start position:

1 Support the barbell across the top of the shoulders on the fleshy part. Use a padded bar or place a towel under the bar to cushion it if necessary. Use an over-grasp (knuckles on top) grip and space the hands wide enough for stability.
2 Keep the back in neutral alignment.
3 The weight should be maintained centrally across the shoulders – imagine a line drawn through the centre of the shoulders and hips.
4 Focus on maintaining the exercise's loading on the front leg.

Action:

5 Bend the knees and hips, dropping the buttocks towards the ground to lower the weight.
6 Lower to an angle of 60–90 degrees at the knee of the front leg.

7 Extend the knees and hips of the front leg to push back up to the start position.

Training tips:

- Maintain a balanced, elevated chest position throughout the exercise.
- When lowering the weight, ensure that the knee of the front leg remains behind its ankle and does not pass (wobble) inside or outside of it, as this could place strain on the joint.
- If using a heavy weight, perform the exercise from under a squat rack.

Exercise 4.5	Split Squat with Dumbbells

Split squat with dumbbells: Holding dumbbells at arms' length by the sides offers a perfectly safer variation, but the athlete needs to be mindful of keeping these in a relatively stable position to maintain exercise integrity. Although some arm movement is inevitable, as long as this is kept to a minimum it could actually be beneficial to the performer as it increases the spatial awareness and balance aspects required (valuable sports performance skills).

Sport-specific Exercise Progression

Exercise 4.6 Split Squat Jump

Split squat jump: This variation adds real dynamic power to the exercise and boosts its relevance to similarly dynamic sports. Assume the same starting position as for the weights version. This time, after lowering the body, drive up powerfully with the front leg to lift the body into the air. While airborne, reverse leg position and land in the split squat position to immediately leap into another jump. This should be achieved without undue yielding of the front thigh. Land 'light' on the feet, towards the forefoot area and on the toes of the rear leg. The arms should be used to assist the jump; this is achieved by first swinging them back and then through and in front of the hips on landing, to add momentum. At the highest point of the jump, the arms should be held straight up on either side of the head.

Training tip: If the athlete is new to this exercise, the strength requirement can be reduced by landing and jumping from a narrower stance. Coincidentally, this increases the speed component. Note: the narrow landing split squat jump is an exercise in its own right and should not be just for beginners. Try combining both variants into workouts.

Exercise 4.7 Single-leg Squat

This exercise should initially be performed with body weight to master technique before adding weight.

Muscles involved: Main quadriceps, secondary hip flexors

Sports applicability: All sports, particularly running

Conditioning benefits:

- *General:* The single-leg squat is a real (and better) alternative to the barbell squat. Even without added weight the exercise develops real strength (and with no weight to support through the back, there is no danger of back injury).
- *Sport-specific:* The single-leg squat is one of the most effective sport-specific resistance conditioning exercises around. This is because most sports skills are performed with an alternate/independent leg action – running is the obvious example. The single-leg squat therefore develops this independent strength. This will:
  - permit the development of more symmetrical leg strength;
  - integrate the core (abdominal and back muscles) into the movement in a way that is highly complementary to sports performance;
  - develop balance – another key sports skill.

Start position:

1 Stand straight, with body weight supported on the right foot. This foot should be flat on the floor; the athlete may need to 'grip' the floor with their toes for stability. The heel of the left foot should be tucked up behind them, with the lower leg approximately parallel to the ground.
2 Look straight ahead and maintain neutral spine position.
3 Keep the arms by the sides.

Action:

4 Bend the knee and hips to lower the buttocks towards the floor. Keep the chest lifted.
5 Lower to the point where it becomes difficult to maintain balance; pause and push back up to return to the start position – ensure this is achieved with control.
6 Ensure that the action of the knee joint occurs in a straight plane while lowering and rising; there should be little lateral movement. Also,

make sure that the knee does not travel beyond the toes. These pointers will minimise knee injury.

Training tips: To aid balance, the athlete may need to 'dab' the floor with their non-supported foot. Fixing their gaze straight ahead and really focusing on the dynamics of the exercise will serve a similar purpose.

Variations

Single-leg squat with hold: The athlete assumes the same starting position as above, but this time lowers deliberately to a three-quarter squat and holds this for 10 seconds before pushing back up to the starting position. The interim static (hopefully!) position should focus the athlete's mind and muscles on stabilisation, which will strengthen the muscles and joints in a way that will combat potential sport-induced injuries. Perform 10 repetitions on each leg.

Added difficulty (and further strength development) can be achieved by using a medicine ball held over the chest or overhead, or by using a barbell across the shoulders or dumbbells held at arms' length by the sides.

| Exercise 4.8 | Single-leg Squat with Hold (Medicine Ball) |

Step-up

Muscles involved: Quadriceps, hamstrings, hip flexors, gastrocnemius, soleus

Sports applicability: All sports, particularly running

Conditioning benefits:

- *General:* The step-up is often overlooked in favour of the squat. It is an advanced exercise, particularly when heavy weights are used, and therefore this version should be performed only by the well-conditioned/advanced athlete.
- *Sport-specific:* There is a school of thought that crowns the step-up as the 'king' of sports conditioning leg weights exercises. This reflects the independent leg action and the movement of the legs, which closely resembles the way the major leg muscles work in harmony to move the body when running and jumping.

Start position:

1 Remove the bar from its stand (this should be set to allow the bar to be removed at shoulder height). Place the weight across the back of the shoulders. Use a padded bar or place a towel under the bar to cushion it against the neck, if necessary. Use an overgrasp (knuckles on top) grip with the hands spaced wide enough for stability.
2 Stand tall and keep the back in neutral position.
3 Feet should be shoulder-width apart with toes pointing straight ahead or slightly turned out.
4 Keep the ankles, knees and hips in alignment.

Action:

5 Step up onto a suitably strong bench by placing the foot of the stepping leg flat on it. The bench should be high enough to allow the athlete to step up from a 90-degree or greater angle of knee bend. The closer the angle is to 90 degrees, the greater the contribution of the hamstring muscles to the exercise.
6 Remove the non-stepping leg from the floor and bring it forwards and up, placing its foot on the bench parallel to the stepping foot and shoulder-width apart.
7 Step back down with the stepping foot to complete one repetition.

Training tip: The athlete should make sure that they step up and down in a straight and balanced line. Failure to do so could strain the ankle, hip, knee and back.

Variations and Sport-specific Exercise Progression

Step-up drive (with or without barbell): This variation is particularly relevant to athletes in dynamic running and jumping sports. It should be performed in one smooth movement. Begin the exercise as described above, but on stepping up onto the bench, 'drive' the non-stepping thigh upwards so that it reaches a position parallel to the floor. At the same time extend up onto the toes of the stepping leg. Next, place the non-stepping leg's foot back down onto the bench and then step back down to the floor as described above. Note: this exercise should be performed dynamically, so only a light weight should be used. Note also: the desire to add speed to the exercise should not be achieved at the expense of technique.

Grounded leg, free-standing step-up drive: This progression is great for developing power-endurance in the quadriceps of the stepping leg. For this exercise the stepping leg is left 'grounded' on the bench throughout the exercise (hence its name). The step-up drive is initiated from the extension of the grounded thigh from the bench and the up-swing of the non-stepping thigh to a position parallel to the ground. The athlete should co-ordinate the movement of their arms and legs in an opposite arm-to-leg running action. Weight can be added, either by using dumbbells held at arms' length or through a barbell supported across the shoulders.

Exercise 4.9	**Step-up Drive**

The following exercises are for more sport-specific core strengthening. More dynamic versions can be found on pages 63–4 (*see also* Table 4.1 for some examples using weights).

Exercise 4.10 The Plank

The plank involves a held isometric contraction of the core. Although most sports do not require such a prolonged or static hold, this exercise will provide a great foundation on which to build more specific core strength.

Assume a type of press-up position, with the weight supported on the forearms. The hands should be placed together in front of the chin (knuckles against knuckles) and the body lifted from the floor. This position should be held to achieve the plank. Start with a 10-second hold and progress as fitness improves.

Core Strength

A strong core (stomach and back) will protect the athlete against injury and serve a vital role in ensuring that power generated by the limbs is not wasted or dissipated in unwanted lateral movements.

Exercise 4.11 Lying Bent Knee Side-to-side Torso Twist

Lie on the ground in a crucifix position with the palms of the hands against the ground. Bring the knees into the chest so that the thighs are at a right angle to the ground and the lower legs parallel to it. Keeping the upper back against the ground, rotate left and right. Hold the legs in position throughout. Just as the legs are about to contact the ground on each twist, pull them 'back and over' to the other side. As the athlete gains proficiency, the speed of the movement can be increased. The arrest and pull-back of the trunk on each twist invokes a plyometric response in the outer torso muscles.

Table 4.1	Further Examples of How to Channel Weight-training Exercises from the General to the More Sport-specific			
Sport	General exercise	Specific exercise	Brief exercise description (specific exercise where needed)	Explanation and sports applicability
Rotational athletic throws, benefits for racket sports. General core strength for all sports.	Latt pulldown	Cable chop	This exercise uses a high pulley machine and a triangular attachment. The athlete should stand facing forward with feet slightly beyond shoulder-width apart. They should hold the attachment with both hands, over their right shoulder, then pull the cable across their body to just beyond their left hip. The exercise can also be performed from a kneeling position and should be performed on both sides to develop symmetrical strength.	A great exercise for developing the functional strength needed for many sports involving trunk rotation. The exercise will also develop rigidity in the core that will buffer unwanted rotational movement for most sports, thus improving power transference.
As above	No real general exercise	Reverse trunk twist	The athlete lies face down on a weights bench, having positioned a barbell across the back of their shoulders, with a training partner holding their ankles	The benefits of this exercise are similar to the one above, although the focus is on the rear torso

Table 4.1	Further Examples of How to Channel Weight-training Exercises from the General to the More Sport-specific cont.			
Sport	General exercise	Specific exercise	Brief exercise description (specific exercise where needed)	Explanation and sports applicability
			down. They rotate their torso left and right, while keeping their hips in contact with the bench. Some gyms may have specialist equipment designed for this exercise.	
Sprints/jumps, and other running- and jumping-based sports (e.g. basketball)	Squat/leg press	Overhead barbell/ powerbag* walk	The athlete holds a light barbell/ powerbag at arms' length overhead and steps forwards with their right leg, cycling their left leg in an 'out and back' clawing motion under their body. Placing their left foot on the ground, they continue forwards by cycling the right leg beneath them as just described. Continue over 15m.	This exercise will develop a solid and straight core – a necessity for optimising power transference between the upper and lower body when running. It will also assist the patterning of the running action leg movement and strengthen the lower legs and ankles.

* Powerbags are sand-filled vinyl tubes with handles. They can be thrown or carried and are used by numerous top sports teams and athletes in their conditioning. For further information contact Performance Technology UK, phone (07941) 040013, e-mail mail@performt.com or visit their website at www.performt.com

Sports Training Tip

The athlete should do some 'muscle re-education' work after their weight-training. For example, a cyclist could do three minutes on a spin cycle after weight-lifting. The sport-specific task will re-coordinate the firing patterns of the muscle cells. A runner could do the same by performing some light strides (medium-paced runs over 60 metres) after a weights workout.

Sports Training Tip:

If you are an athlete, be mindful that you don't become a gym narcissist and marvel at your 'great physique' brought about by weight-training. It could become no more than a suit of armour for you to haul around with you (see 'Power-to-weight Ratio', page 56).

Weight-training for Endurance

In the past, weight-training was often eschewed by endurance athletes for fear that it would work against improved performance, with some foundation (*see* 'Training for Endurance and Weight-training – the Interference Effect', page 130). However, it is now accepted that the 'right' weight-training programme (coupled with the 'right' power-training programme) should form a major part of the endurance athlete's training plan, if not as a direct contributor to improving endurance activity, at least as a pre-conditioner. (Circuit training methods, often associated with endurance training, are covered below.)

Everything else being equal, a larger, stronger muscle will be more fatigue-resistant.

Sports Training Tip

Certain types of weight-training, notably low-repetition, high-load methods (maximum strength weight-training), have little direct relevance to improving endurance performance. However, low-load, high-repetition methods, such as circuit resistance training, are relevant.

Sports Circuit Training Methods

Circuit training (CT) offers the athlete and coach a myriad of possibilities. It is possible to design circuits with ever-increasing degrees of sport specificity. Options range from general strength endurance to speed development, tennis agility and goal-keeping fitness. The scope and design is very much dependent on the creativity of the coach. Despite this, circuits are generally seen as being useful for 'base/foundation' condition and for endurance athletes. Consequently, they are often included in the early stages of the training plan/year. In this section, I provide examples of circuits for a wide variety of sports and times in the training calendar. This will enable athlete/coach to see how applicable this training method is to a wide variety of sports-conditioning requirements.

Local Muscular Strength Endurance

Most circuits are designed to develop local muscular endurance – the ability of a muscle or muscle group to perform repeated contractions under fatigued conditions. This usually places medium to high levels of stress on the body's overall system, notably in terms of an elevated cardiovascular response. Note: It is possible to develop aerobic capacity via CT (see page 132).

The Basic Components of a Circuit

All circuits are comprised of:

- **Exercises:** weights, body weight, speed, strength, agility or skill-based;
- **Repetitions:** traditionally high to promote strength endurance;
- **Periods of rest and recovery:** kept short to promote local muscular strength endurance and aerobic/anaerobic fitness.

Making Circuits More Sport-specific

By playing around with the rest and repetition components of CT, coach/athlete can induce a more or less fatiguing effect on the athlete. Regardless of this, it is always best to select exercises that reflect the movement patterns of the sport being trained for. A sprinter might, for example, complete a quality circuit to enhance speed and neuromuscular response.

Sports Training Tip

Rest is the most important training variable when it comes to circuit design. This can be adjusted to promote circuits of different qualities that will be more or less fatiguing.

Examples of Sport-specific Circuit Training

Coach and athlete should use the examples provided to create their own relevant performance-improving circuits, which can be shaped to fit all stages of the training year.

Understanding Training Planning

Training phases are referred to as 'microcycles', 'mesocycles' and 'macrocycles' in 'periodised' training plans. Respectively, these are simply short-, medium- and long-term training periods, each of which has a different emphasis. As an example, a macrocycle could last for three months and contain three month-long mesocycles, each containing four one-week microcycles. Training would be adjusted across these cycles, depending on the emphasis of each, to develop every opportunity for improving sport-specific condition. Microcycles are the actual workouts, the detail to the more general strategies and emphases placed in the longer meso- and macrocycles. For more information on training planning, turn to part 8.

Rowing Circuit

Develops: Strength and specific local muscular endurance relevant to race-rowing heart rates
Components: Weight and body weight exercises
Time of training year: Pre-competition phase mesocycle
Comment: Designed by Olympic rowing coach Terry O'Neill who believes that a weight-training programme for rowing should mirror, as closely as possible, race requirements. He bases his circuit on the ultimate goal of the rower – completing the 2km distance as fast as possible. This means that:

- the exercises selected must be relevant to rowing;
- they must ultimately be performed at a pace equivalent to actual stroke rate;
- they must create conditions that mirror the heart rate and lactate levels sustained during a 2km race;
- they must reflect the time it takes to complete the race distance.

O'Neill outlines his ideas behind the positioning of this circuit in the pre-competition mesocycle as follows: 'In this mesocycle the weight is reduced from previous mesocycles. This is so that the athlete can complete 45 seconds of continuous rhythmic exercise at a given rate at each station (exercise). At the end of each station the athlete moves on to the next without stopping. This gives a total of eight minutes' work, during which time the heart rate will rise to 85–95 per cent HRMax. I get the athletes to rest for two minutes at the end of each complete circuit. The aim is for them to do three complete circuits during the first three weeks, and four in weeks four, five and six of the mesocycle.'

It appears logical that the transfer from this type of circuit to actual 2km rowing would be considerable. This type of circuit – with changes to rest, recovery, number of circuits and weight lifted (where appropriate) – could also be tailored to other phases of a rower's preparations. For example, at the beginning of the training year/period, the number of circuits and weight lifted would be increased gradually as the rower regains condition, permitting over time the performance of faster, more powerful and demanding versions, like the one described, as the competitive season draws near.

Level of resistance: For all exercises the weight (where appropriate) is kept to 15–30kg to enable the speed component of the lift/exercise to remain high and closely match the rowing stroke.

Go to http://www.concept2.co.uk to find out more about indoor and outdoor rowing and weight-training.

The Exercises

- High pull

- Press behind neck

- Biceps curl

- Bent-over rowing

- Side bends to right and left

- Squat (Single/Double)

- Bench press

- Clean and press

- Crunch

- Bench pull

- Hyper-extensions

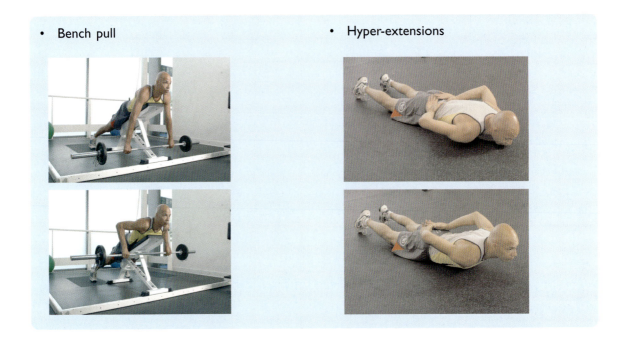

Speed Conditioning Base
Strength Leg Circuit

Develops: Strength and specific local muscular endurance relevant to sprinting

Components: Body weight exercises, plus specialised exercises using 5kg weight disc

Time of training year: Preparatory macrocycles (early season)

Comment: Used by Malcolm Arnold, coach to 4 x 100m Olympic champion Jason Gardener and retired high hurdles world champion and world record holder, Colin Jackson. The number of repetitions and circuits is gradually increased during the initial training mesocycles. The mix of exercises reflects the single-leg sprinting movement. Some exercises are performed at high speed, which again provides every opportunity for a conditioning-to-performance match.

The Exercises

- Forward lunge to Backward lunge

- Sideways lunge

- Running on the spot, with parallel to ground straight-knee lift

- Running on the spot, with parallel to ground angled-knee lift

- Running on the spot, parallel to ground knee lift, holding a weight disc at arms' length parallel to the floor

The time of each exercise and number of circuits are gradually increased as the athlete's fitness improves. There is no recovery between exercises; between circuits a recovery time of one to two minutes is used.

Plyometric Circuit

Develops: Strength and specific plyometric local muscular endurance, relevant to sprinters and jumpers, and basketball, volleyball and tennis players

Components: Dynamic (jumping) body weight exercises

Time of training year: General preparation macrocycle, but can be adjusted for use during the competition-specific macrocycle, with much reduced repetitions and longer recoveries

Comment: I used variations of this circuit myself as a long jump athlete and have used it with other power athletes. I stress that each exercise should be performed with as much quality as possible. If the athlete becomes too fatigued then they risk conditioning a too slow plyometric response and injury.

The Exercises

• Straight-leg jumps

• Split jumps

• Squat jumps with hand on hips

- Abdominal crunch (to break up the plyometric exercises)

- Tuck jumps

I tend to operate this circuit on a 'set number of repetitions' basis, for example, 15 repetitions of each exercise. I then use a recovery of one to two minutes between circuits, depending on the athlete's condition and the time in the training year. For example, if I was using the circuit closer to the competition season, I would add a 10-second recovery between exercises and instruct the athlete to be as fast as possible in terms of their ground contacts. The number of circuits would be reduced accordingly.

Kettlebells

Kettlebells offer unique sports training possibilities for the athlete and coach. Although similar to dumbbells, their unique design – they look like cannonballs with handles on top – and the many exercises that can be performed with them make them particularly relevant to sports conditioning.

Kettlebells have a long history. They originated in the former Soviet Union around the turn of the 20th century, and have now become popular on both sides of the Atlantic. In the UK, top athletes and rugby clubs such as Wasps and the Newcastle Falcons use them. Kettlebells can be lifted, carried, held statically in place and thrown.

Kettlebell training, according to Soviet research, develops strength in totally unrelated tasks such as:

- Grip strength
- Power lifting
- Strength endurance – measured by pull-ups and parallel bar dips
- Balance
- Even a 1000m run

For details of Kettlebells, contact Powerseekers UK, phone (0208) 245 3569, e-mail enquiries@powerseekers.com or visit their website at powerseeker.co.uk

Selected Kettlebell Exercises

The Swing

The swing is a great all-body power exercise. It is also a base Kettlebell move which forms the stem of many others.

Body parts targeted: Back (particularly lower), legs (particularly hamstrings), forearm and grip

How to perform the exercise: With the feet shoulder-width apart, the athlete holds the Kettlebell handle with two hands at arms' length in front of their legs. The eyes should be fixed on an elevated point in the distance. The athlete 'snaps' their hips through by explosively contracting their buttock muscles and lifts through the thighs, making the Kettlebell rise. The Kettlebell is then lifted with the arms extended in front of the body. The height of the swing may vary – anywhere between waist to above the head is fine. As the Kettlebell is lowered, the abs are tightened to absorb the momentum by giving slightly at the knees and thighs.

Training tip: To really swing the Kettlebell, power must be generated simultaneously through the legs and hips. However, confidence should be gained with lower swings before progressing to higher ones.

Swing Variations

Single-hand swing: Perform the single-hand swing in exactly the same way as the double-hand version, but with only one hand. This exercise is relevant to those involved in combat and racket sports.

Wide-stance swing: Use two Kettlebells, one in each hand. Start from a wide-leg position (feet approximately one-and-a-half times shoulder-width apart). This variant places a different emphasis on the limbs. Swing the Kettlebells from inside the legs. Watch your knees on the way back down!

Sports Training Tip

Athletes in contact sports can develop greater resistance to hits and punches through the use of resistance training equipment such as Kettlebells and powerbags. Both items can be thrown and can 'hit' the body during conditioning exercises. This will boost body resilience, a highly relevant 'skill' for those involved in these sports.

Weight-training and Hormonal Response

Most coaches and athletes will appreciate the 'external' physical changes that occur through weight-training, such as potentially increased muscle size, muscular power and strength endurance. However, they may be far less familiar with the effects weight-training can have on the hormonal (endocrine) system and the consequences.

Charles Van Commenee (the former coach to Olympic heptathlon gold medallist Denise Lewis) advocated the use of maximum strength weight-training workouts, using weights in excess of 90 per cent of 1 repetition maximum (1RM). These were to be performed in numerous sets (eight plus) using full recoveries. This contrasts with the 70–80 per cent of 1RM fast movement power workouts (employing six to eight fast movement repetitions over three to six sets) often used by the sprinter/jumper athlete.

Van Commenee's reasoning was that the latter type of workout was more of a body-builder's one, designed to produce an increased anabolic hormonal – notably growth hormone (GH) – workout response, which would build more muscle. Van Commenee considered that a higher-intensity, greater GH-releasing workout might increase an athlete's weight sufficiently to compromise performance. However, the

heavier, low-repetition workout, although developing crucial athletic power, was less likely to do so. Van Commenee's opinions are no doubt based on numerous sports science studies that vindicate his stance (*see*, for example, *Sports Med.*, 2005; 35(4): 339–61). Consequently, Van Commenee balanced his athletes' weight-training sessions in order to create the requisite power and size needed for optimum performance.

The Case for Increasing Muscle Mass

As I indicated previously, there are instances when an athlete may wish to increase their lean muscle mass in order to enhance sports performance. Rugby players, for example, will need to maintain bulk to be at their most effective. For these athletes, high-intensity 'power' weights workouts are entirely appropriate, as they will assist the process of maintaining and developing larger muscles through their anabolic and hormonal effects.

The key for athlete/coach when planning a weight-training schedule is not only to take into account the perceived benefits of the session per se on muscle fibre response, but also its hormonal response and the way that this can influence an athlete's weight.

Other Hormonal Weight-training Consequences

I have provided more information on weight-training's hormonal effects, as they can have crucial consequences on the training of female and master athletes, for example.

Age, Sex and Hormone Release

Scientists from the University of North Carolina noted that GH secretion varied with regard to age and sex. They discovered that the magnitude of GH release was greater in young women than in young men, and perhaps less surprisingly, was reduced four- to seven-fold in older individuals compared to their younger counterparts. It therefore seems that the late teens and early twenties are a good time to boost lean muscle mass in female athletes, as their bodies appear more responsive to hormonally stimulated, weight-training-induced muscle growth (*see also* part 1, page 15 for the best time to train physical qualities).

Age and GH Secretion for Master Athletes

The researchers also noted that the age-related drop in GH secretion was often associated with deleterious health effects, although a cause and effect relationship was not established. The good news is that while sports training and exercise interventions may not restore GH secretion to the levels observed in the young, exercise is still a robust stimulus for GH secretion. The implications of this for the master athlete are relatively obvious: where possible, intense weight-training should be performed to naturally spike (increase) GH levels. This will contribute towards maintaining lean muscle mass, which declines significantly with age. Table 4.2 (*see* page 90) contains selected weight-training workouts and their specific hormonal consequences. (Reference: *Sports Med., 2002;* 32(15): 987–1004)

Testosterone, Age, Sex and Weight-training

Research by Finnish scientists examined the relationship between age and sex and weight-training-induced testosterone release. Forty-two subjects were divided into four groups:

1 10 middle-aged men (average age 42)
2 11 middle-aged women (average age 39)
3 11 elderly men (average age 72)
4 10 elderly women (average age 67)

The study consisted of six months' heavy resistance training and explosive exercises and produced interesting results. Functional training response was improved significantly: 1RM values increased in the middle-aged men by 27 per cent; in the elderly men by 16 per cent; in the middle-aged women by 28 per cent and in the elderly women   by 24 per cent. Training stimulated a significant testosterone response in both male groups, but not in the female groups. GH levels, on the other hand, increased in all groups, except the oldest women. In terms of providing an explanation for the latter, the researchers noted that, 'The physiological significance of the lack of acute responsiveness of GH to heavy resistance exercise in older women . . . during prolonged strength training requires further examination.' However, these findings again demonstrate the value of weight-training for a positive hormonal response in the older athlete and females. (Reference: *Gerontol. A Biol. Sci. Med. Sci.,* 2000 Feb; 55(2): B95–105)

Table 4.2	Suggested Workouts – Weight-training: Selected Sports and Hormonal Response	
Target group	**Workout aim**	**Suggested workout**
Young women (late teens, early 20s) – long, triple, high jumpers, basketball players, volleyball and tennis players	To promote powerful lean muscle	4 x 8 fast @ 80% 1RM – slightly incomplete recovery (power method)
Men (sports as above)	To promote powerful lean muscle	4 x 8 fast @ 80% 1RM – slightly incomplete recovery (power method)
Men/women (sports as above)	To promote power/strength without building too much muscle	10 x 1 @ 95% 1RM – full recovery (max strength method)
Master athletes – male (sports as above)	To promote muscle maintenance and power	1) 4 x 8 fast @ 75% 1RM – full recovery (power method) 2) 4 x 2 @ 90% 1RM*
Master athletes – female (sports as above)	To promote muscle maintenance and power	1) 4 x 10 fast @ 70%1RM – slightly incomplete 2) 4 x 2 @ 90% 1RM* (power method)
Master and endurance athletes**	Primary purpose to promote muscle maintenance	4 x 10 fast @ 70% 1RM – slightly incomplete recovery* (power method)

All these programmes target the elevation of GH and testosterone. Each workout should consist of exercises that recruit large muscle groups.

* Regular intense endurance training can reduce muscle mass due to its catabolic effect on muscle protein.
** Both master and endurance athlete need to combat both training and age-related declines, hence the reason for this workout. There are complications when weight-training and endurance training at the same time (see 'Training for Endurance and Weight-training – the Interference Effect', page 130).

Hormones, the Endocrine System and Weight-training

Physiologists refer to hormones as 'chemical messengers'. They are produced by the endocrine system and endocrine glands, such as the hypothalamus in the brain and the gonads. The system influences the body in a multitude of ways, ranging from metabolism to growth and mood. As previously mentioned, the endocrine system works hand in hand with the nervous system.

The major function of hormones is to change the rates of specific reactions in target cells. A cell's response to a hormone is determined by the presence of certain protein receptors in its membrane or interior. Muscle fibres, like the rest of the body, are constituted from cells, and the way a hormone interacts with these can significantly affect training adaptation. The hormonal contribution involves a complex physiological response, but ultimately results in the DNA-mediated synthesis of new contractile proteins, which are vital to muscle cell function and integrity.

Growth Hormone (GH)

GH is released from the anterior pituitary gland in the brain soon after exercise commences. GH is regarded as the 'sport hormone' because it is involved in numerous anabolic (growth) functions relating to cell proliferation and division throughout the body. Specifically, GH stimulates bone, cartilage and muscle growth, and can play a very significant role in lean muscle mass and fat deterioration/accumulation. GH release via exercise is augmented by a further chemical reaction. Basically, hormones that would otherwise act to blunt GH production (such as somatostatin) are suppressed by the production of other chemicals produced during exercise (endogenous opiates). In short, GH's ergogenic (boosting) training-induced effect can contribute towards creating a leaner, stronger, more powerful athlete.

Testosterone

Testosterone is produced in men through the testes and in women, to a much lesser extent, via the ovaries. The primary role of testosterone is to augment the release of GH and to interact with the nervous system. Hormones can affect mood and behaviour. An increased level of testosterone could, for example, result in greater feelings of aggression/dominance through 'interpretation' by the nervous system and brain. The mechanisms behind this process (and other hormonal influences on behaviour) are complex.

Cortisol

Cortisol is released from the adrenal glands and its levels are elevated by exercise. It stimulates protein breakdown, leading to the creation of energy in the form of glucose in the liver. This is not so good for athletes looking to build (and maintain) muscle, as amino acids (released via dietary protein breakdown, see page 193) become preferentially used for energy production rather than muscle building.

It should also be noted that high hormone levels can affect cellular response negatively as well as positively. Too great a hormonal stimulus can desensitise cells, reducing their ability to adapt positively (this is called 'down regulation'). Athletes should bear this in mind, especially when considering cortisol.

PART **FIVE**

DEVELOPING POWER

The manifestation of power in sport makes for an awesome sight. An elite male sprinter can reach speeds close to 30mph, and a basketball player seems to be able to stop the clock with their 'hang time' while performing a slam dunk or similar skill. Cricket deliveries zing around batsmen's ears at more than 100mph, while tennis serves singe the net at even greater velocities. Practising the key elements of the athlete's sport and/or sprinting at maximum or at over speed (*see* page 151) will improve an athlete's power and speed. However, to achieve even higher velocities and greater levels of power, more specific conditioning exercises are required. In this part I describe some of the most effective of these training methods. This part should be read in conjunction with part 7, 'Developing Speed and Agility'.

Plyometric Exercises

Plyometric (jumping/dynamic-type) exercises are key to the development of athletic power and are relevant to the majority of sports. Plyometrics may or may not be combined with weights exercises into a workout specifically designed to boost fast twitch muscle fibre output – this is known as 'power combination training' (*see* page 105).

Plyometric Muscular Action

Plyometric muscular contractions release incredible amounts of force in a split second. This 'concentric following eccentric muscular contraction' (*see* part 1, page 13) is crucial to speed and power in a highly sport-specific way. This type of contraction happens every time a runner's foot hits the ground, or when a rower drives hard into and out of the stroke (at the catch). As these examples indicate, plyometric exercises have a role to play in training for the majority of sports. Endurance athletes and coaches take note: plyometrics are not just for speed athletes.

Why are Plyometrics Best for Speed and Power?

Plyometric exercises closely reflect the speed of movement and the movement patterns of numerous sports and sports skills. Unlike traditional weight-training exercises, plyometric drills closely reflect both the movement pattern and the speed of execution of actual sports performance and allow great forces to be overcome, many times the athlete's weight.

With plyometrics, athletes can match sport-specific ground-contact times (*see* Table 5.1) and generate incredible force at the same time. One piece of Soviet research showed that, under certain conditions, athletes could display brief (0.037–0.067 seconds) plyometrically-induced muscular tensions, equivalent to 1500–3500kg! Although this example was probably based on eccentric plyometric drills (such as 'drop and hold' depth jumps from a great height) rather than more commonly used eccentric to concentric muscular action, hopping and bounding exercises, it is easy to understand why they are a great tool in the conditioning armoury.

Table 5.1	Ground Contact Activity and Foot Contact Times/Force	
Ground contact activity	Time of foot contact (sec)	Force (kg)
Sprinting	0.90	477
Bounding	0.175	545
Long jump take-off	0.110	623
Depth jump (40cm drop)	0.200	450
Hopping	0.180	265

Adapted from G. Dintiman and B. Ward, *Sports Speed* (third edition), Human Kinetics, 2003

Improvements in Performance Economy

Plyometric training can also improve the body's natural energy return system. Using running as an example, every time the foot strikes the ground, the muscles and tendons of the ankle, lower and upper leg all stretch and store energy. On 'push-off' into the next stride, this stored energy helps to propel the athlete forwards. In fact, it is estimated that 90 per cent of the energy produced from this storage is returned. At first glance this appears extremely positive as, compared with other animals, humans are very efficient running machines. But it is *because* of this efficiency that our running muscles (of the calf, thigh and hips) often work well within their capabilities when contributing to the running stride. Plyometric training can increase the power available from the athlete's muscles (particularly from fast twitch muscle fibre). This will provide every opportunity for a more effective expression of speed and optimum running economy.

Understanding Plyometric Power

What happens when you throw a rubber ball against a wall? It springs back. If you throw it harder, it returns faster. Plyometric training will increase the 'hardness' of the athlete's muscular reactions, which will make them speedier and more dynamic.

Sports Training Tip

The development of power, speed and agility is intertwined. Coach and athlete must be aware of all the options that are available, and the implications of the different training methods, when planning a programme designed to improve power and speed.

Plyometric Training Tips

1   Always warm up specifically (*see* part 3).
2   Train on a non-slip surface; a running track or sports hall floor are ideal but a dry, flat, grass surface will also do.
3   Wear well-cushioned and supportive trainers.
4   Maintain neutral spine position, where applicable – looking straight ahead will help achieve this (*see* page 60).
5   For leg exercises, land 'light' towards the forefoot (not on tiptoes).
6   Do not bend the knees excessively to absorb the impact of each landing; rather, react as quickly as possible to the ground from a relatively straight leg position, as this will maximise the plyometric effect and improve joint stiffness and energy return.
7   When performing upper-body plyometrics (especially when the hands, arms and shoulders absorb the impact), work in a controlled manner and avoid strain by mastering technique before increasing speed.
8   Always underestimate what can be achieved to start with and select less demanding (but no less effective) exercises (*see* Table 5.2). It will take a while for the athlete's body to become used to the impact forces involved.
9   Do not perform intense plyometric workouts close to important competitions – keep at least five days clear.
10 Pre-condition. Weight-training is crucial in this respect as it will strengthen soft tissue, making it less prone to strain whilst providing a base for plyometric power to be built on.

Sports Training Tip

Coach/athlete should allow long rest periods between plyometric exercises – and sets of exercises – to get the most from them unless they are looking to promote power endurance, when shorter recoveries will be more relevant (see page 85).

For speed development, 30–60 seconds' recovery should be taken between repetitions – and 2–3 minutes between sets. This will avoid fatiguing fast twitch muscle fibres, enabling them to contribute maximum force to each effort/set.

Sports Training Tip

Plyometric training for speed should stop when the athlete becomes fatigued and movement slow – there is no point in conditioning a slow reaction.

Selected Plyometric Exercises

In this section I describe a variety of plyometric exercises. I have provided a difficulty/intensity rating for each, indicated in Table 5.2. Suggested repetitions and sets are provided, but these are for guideline purposes only.

Lower-body Plyometrics

Exercise 5.1	Straight-leg Jumps

This exercise is suitable for all running and jumping sports. Stand with feet shoulder-width apart. Take the arms back and bend the knees slightly. Using predominantly the ankles and calf muscles, jump into the air. Swing the arms down and past the hips at the same time to increase power. On landing, react as quickly as possible to the ground, again primarily using the feet, ankles and calf muscles. Do three sets of ten repetitions.

Exercise 5.2 Standing Jumps from Side to Side

Variation: Stand to one side of a line and jump from side to side of it, with the lower legs providing most of the power. This exercise will pre-condition and improve lower-limb and ankle agility, a useful attribute for field and racket sport players who have to make dynamic turns and cutting movements. Do 3 sets of 10 repetitions.

Exercise 5.3 Spring Jogging

This exercise will improve running foot strike, and is suitable for runners of all speeds and running-based sports. Start jogging, and after a few metres begin to generate more bounce on each stride. Use the ankles, and the upper and lower legs to push upwards and forwards while maintaining a running arm action. Do 3 x 30m.

Depth Jumps

Stand on top of a strong step or box (40–80cm high). Maintaining neutral spine position and looking straight ahead, step off the box, land on the forefeet and immediately spring back up into the air. Do not allow the upper thighs to bend too much on impact. The arms should be swung back as the athlete steps off the box and forwards and up just before rebounding to aid speed and power.

The greater the height of the step or box (within the confines mentioned above), the greater the strength component of the exercise; the lower the height, the greater the speed component. A speed/power training programme for most sports should include examples of both. However, the athlete should always emphasise ground contact and speed of reaction. Do four sets of six repetitions.

Sports Training Tip

Depth jump session volume is usually measured by the number of ground contacts performed in a workout. The athlete should avoid doing more than 60 and no more than two to three workouts a week. Note: there are exceptions to this, such as when training for power endurance (see page 85).

Exercise 5.4   Depth Jumps

Exercise 5.5 Bounding

Exercise 5.6 Hopping

Stand facing the direction of bounding. To start, leap forwards to land on one leg. The landing should be made towards the forefoot. On ground contact, immediately leap forwards on to the other leg. This should be achieved by attempting to stay in the air for as long as possible. The arms should be coordinated with the legs – opposite arm to leg for a 'single-arm shift' movement – or pulled back together behind the body and brought through and forwards on and through each ground contact for a 'double-arm shift'. Note: The latter technique is best employed by field athletes whose sports, such as the high jump and triple jump, use the double-arm shift at takeoff.

The double-arm action should also be used when performing double-leg jumps, such as tuck and bunny/squat jumps.

Hops are performed from one leg at a time and are consequently more intense than bounds. Stand facing the direction of hopping, with the chest elevated. Bend the hopping leg slightly and push back against the ground to generate the force needed to hop. Land flat-footed/on the forefeet, without unduly yielding at the knee, then spring immediately into another hop. The hopping leg should be cycled in the air, under and brought through to a position in front of the athlete's body as they progress from hop to hop.

Do no more than 15–20 repetitions of hops and bounds over a distance of 10–20m in sets of four to five.

Speed Hops and Bounds

Hopping and bounding exercises can also be performed with more speed and with less emphasis on the hold and in-air part of the movement (with or without a run-up). These speed hops and bounds are even more speed-specific as they reduce ground contact time. The athlete should aim to strike the ground as fast and dynamically as possible. These exercises should be performed over 20–30m, ideally with performances timed to monitor progress.

Speed hops and bounds are very specific to sprinting and the off-the-spot acceleration needed for racket and field sports, if a standing start is used.

Upper-body Plyometrics

Plyometric exercises can be performed for the core (abdominals and back) and shoulders/arms. Many of these exercises involve throwing medicine balls or powerbags.

Plyometric Press-up

Exercise 5.7 Plyometric Press-up

Assume a normal press-up position. Lower the body and drive the arms upwards to 'jump' the body from the floor. On landing, immediately push back into the next press-up. The plyometric response occurs in the shoulders at the transitory point of impact.

Exercise 5.8   Plyometric Press-up (variation)

Variation: Kneel and pivot forwards from the knees to 'fall' towards the floor and perform the exercise as described above.

Do three to four sets of six repetitions. Note: these exercises should not be performed if the athlete has weak wrists or shoulders.

Medicine Ball Sit-up and Throw

The athlete will need the assistance of a coach/training partner to get the most out of this exercise. Take hold of a light medicine ball (2.5kg) and assume a sit-up position, with the feet flat on the floor and knees bent to an angle of 90 degrees. The medicine ball should be held across the chest, with the hands to the sides of it. To throw the medicine ball, lower the back towards the floor then, using the abdominal muscles, pull the trunk forwards dynamically. Near the top of the movement, throw the ball to the coach/partner using a chest pass action by pushing the arms dynamically away. The coach/partner should catch the medicine ball and toss it back, just as the athlete is sitting back ready to perform the next repetition. It is the 'catch and move forwards to throw' part of the exercise that develops the plyometric response in the torso. Do 4 sets of 10 repetitions.

| Exercise 5.9 | **Medicine Ball Sit-up and Throw (variation)** | Exercise 5.10 | **Medicine Ball Pass against a Wall** |

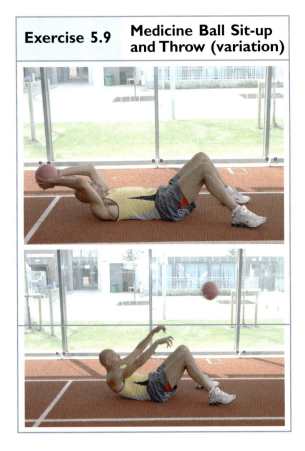

Variation: Perform the exercise in a similar way to described above, but this time throw and catch the ball from an overhead position. Whoever is catching the ball should stand further away, as the athlete will be capable of throwing the medicine ball greater distances than for the previous exercise. Do 4 sets of 10 repetitions.

Both the above exercises lend themselves to measurement and testing.

Stand close to a wall, facing it. Take hold of a medicine ball as if making a chest pass. To perform the throw dynamically, press the medicine ball away. The ball should be caught and immediately thrown back against the wall. The athlete should try to perform the exercise as fast as possible. It is the quick catch and throw action that develops the plyometric action. Do 3 sets of 15 repetitions.

More upper-body plyometric exercises are considered in part 7 in terms of their contribution to agility and rotational speed and power development.

Are Upper-body Plyometric Exercises as Effective as those for the Lower Body?

Research suggests that medicine ball and similar upper-body plyometric drills may be less effective at developing power than lower-body drills or certain selected upper-body plyometric exercises (such as the plyometric press-up). This is because the former do not allow as much force to be overcome as the latter.

Lower-body plyometric exercises, as explained, can produce huge amounts of force – at least three times body weight. The plyometric press-up overcomes only about 30 per cent of the athlete's body weight, together with any additional force that has to be overcome as the height and speed of the movement increases. With medicine ball exercises, however, there is much less power to overcome.

For an athlete looking for an upper-body power boost to improve their throwing, pushing and punching, the plyometric press-up makes the best choice as long as their wrists, arms, shoulders and back are pre-conditioned to stand the force.

Nevertheless, medicine ball drills do still have a role to play in speed and power conditioning. They can, for example, be highly effective at increasing an athlete's neuromuscular response and reaction capability. Throwing heavier and lighter implements, for example by a baseball pitcher or javelin thrower, can have a similar effect.

Making Plyometric Exercises Even More Sports-specific

Plyometric exercises, in the forms described above, offer a specific way to improve speed, power and endurance. However, they can often be made even more specific with the addition of a relevant sports movement, such as a header after a depth jump for a footballer. Here is another example.

Double-footed Depth Jump with 10m Sprint

| Exercise 5.11 | Double-footed Depth Jump with 10m Sprint |

This variation exemplifies just how far a plyometric exercise like the depth jump can be adapted for sport-specific purposes. It is suitable for racket and field sports players and designed to assist the development of explosive acceleration in non-linear directions. To perform the exercise, step off the platform for a two-footed landing. While in the air, 'rotate', so as to land at an angle, such as 45 degrees to the left. On landing, drive (push back) explosively with one leg, while pulling the other through quickly from the hip to accelerate forwards. Continue to accelerate for 10m, concentrating on leg drive and hip pull-through. The arms should be pumped backwards and forwards as vigorously as possible to aid acceleration. Do three sets of eight repetitions, varying the angle of landing and sprint. A racket sport player could even perform the exercise holding a racket.

Table 5.2 Plyometric Drills Ranked by Intensity and Suitability

Type of plyometric exercise	Examples	Intensity
Standing-based jumps performed on the spot	Tuck jumps Split jumps Squat jumps	Low
Jumps from standing	Standing long jump Standing hop Standing jump for height	Low to medium
Medicine ball throws	Chest pass or overhead throw from sit-up position	Low to medium
Multiple jumps from standing	5 consecutive bounds 2 x 6 double-footed jumps Double-footed jumps over 4 hurdles 10 x double-footed jumps up stadium steps	Medium to high

Table 5.2	Plyometric Drills Ranked by Intensity and Suitability cont.	
Type of plyometric exercise	**Examples**	**Intensity**
Multiple jumps with run-up	2 hops and jump into sand pit with 10-stride approach 10 bounds with 8-stride run-up	High
Depth jumping (Recommended drop height 40–80cm – the greater the height the greater the strength component, the lower the height the greater the speed.)	6 jumps – down and up	High
	Run to hop on and off low box on to one-leg landing, followed by 3 subsequent hops	Very high
Eccentric depth jump	Step or hop off a box, as with depth jump, but cushion the impact i.e. do not spring up or forwards into another jump	High
Plyo press-ups	4 x 6	Medium/high

Intensity versus Value

It is important not to confuse intensity with the value of a plyometric exercise. A lower-intensity exercise, such as straight-leg jumps performed on the spot, has no less value than a high-intensity exercise, such as a depth jump. Rather, athlete/coach should use intensity to refer to the amount of force and potential strain the exercise places on the body. All develop the plyometric response and all, irrespective of their intensity, will contribute towards increasing speed.

Power Combination Training

Power combination training describes a power-developing workout that combines weights and plyometric exercises. This can be done in various ways.

Potentiation

The key physiological justification of these workouts revolves around the 'potentiation' effect. Potentiation refers to the influence that one training method can have on another in terms of enhancing the ability of fast twitch muscle fibres to generate greater force. Initially, research focused on the potentiation of the plyometric exercise by a weights one. Note: The exercises involved are 'paired' and work the same muscle groups, for example the squat and squat jump. More recently, however, researchers have looked in the 'other' direction to see whether weight-lifting power could be enhanced by the prior performance of a plyometric exercise.

Power Combination Training Variation

• **Complex training** involves performing sets of related weight-training exercises before sets of plyometric ones. For example, three sets of ten half-squats before three sets of ten jump squats – these are the 'complexes'.
• **Contrast training** involves performing one set of the weights exercise first and then a plyometric one for a given number of sets. For example, one set of ten half-squats followed by one set of ten jump squats, repeated over three sets.

How Heavy should the Weight be for Complex/Contrast Power Combination Training?

It is argued that the weights exercises, for both complex and contrast training workouts, should be in excess of 70 per cent 1RM. This is because a lighter loading is believed to be insufficient to 'hit' type IIb fast twitch muscle fibres sufficiently to cause potentiation.

Sports Training Tip

The athlete should always try to rebound/react/throw as fast and dynamically as possible when performing plyometric exercises. The greater the eccentric contraction, the greater the concentric one will be.

The Effect of Prior Strength Levels on the Success of Power Combination Workouts

Researchers examined jump squat power in complex, contrast and what they call 'traditional' training workouts. Eleven women with different strength levels participated in a familiarisation session and then in three randomly ordered testing sessions. Session one involved completing sets of jump squats before sets of half-squats (traditional method). Session two involved sets of half-squats before jump squats (complex method). Session three involved alternating sets of half-squats and jump squats (contrast method). The research findings indicated no significant enhancement of jump squat performance for the traditional, contrast and complex methods for the lower strength-trained group. However, the team did find that prior levels of strength had an effect. The stronger women had superior jump squat performances as an outcome of the contrast training. Hence it was concluded that contrast training was advantageous for increasing power output, but only for athletes with relatively high prior strength levels. (Reference: *J. Strength Cond. Res.*, 2002 Nov; 16(4): 530–8)

Other research has also indicated the importance of prior strength levels on power combination workout outcomes. This research discovered that pre-squatting significantly enhanced the vertical jumping ability of their survey's stronger participants by 4.01 per cent and that of the weaker group by 0.45 per cent.

(Reference: *J. Strength Cond. Res.* 2003 May; 17(2): 342–4)

In practical terms, this means that the coach must be mindful of the prior strength levels of their athletes and be willing to implement (and experiment) with the ordering of the power combination workout training elements in order to achieve the most significant adaptations. They should also be prepared to vary the loading of the weights exercises (normally between 70–90 per cent of 1RM) and also the number of repetitions (normally between 4 and 10). Recording the results over time will highlight the workouts that produce the best results and the physical attributes of the athlete that may need to be worked on to produce the best potentiation effect and gains.

The Plyometric Potentiation of Weight-training Exercises

As I indicated, most power combination training research has focused on the effect of the weight-training exercise on the plyometric one. However, there is a growing body of research that has looked in the 'other' direction, often with positive results.

Researchers looked at the effect of plyometric exercises on 1RM squat performance. Twelve trained men participated in three testing sessions separated by at least six days of rest. In the first testing session, subjects performed a series of weights sets with increasing loads until their 1RM was determined. During the second and third testing sessions, subjects performed either three double-leg tuck jumps (TJ) or two depth jumps (DJ) 30 seconds before each 1RM attempt. Three 1RM attempts were

allowed and at least four minutes' recovery was taken between each attempt.

The researchers discovered that performing plyometric exercises before going for a 1RM maximum did have a positive effect. Tuck jumps increased the group's collective squat performance to 140.5kg, and prior depth jumping to 144.5kg. With no plyometrics, the group managed only 139.6kg. (Reference: *J. Strength Cond. Res.*, 2001 Nov; 14(4): 470–476)

This is obviously very encouraging news for power and weight-lifters and power/speed athletes looking to increase general muscular strength via weight-training, as it indicates that plyometric potentiation can work. This provides a further power building workout option for coach/athlete. Note: It is also a direct example (as is power combination training in general) of the channelling of power and strength through appropriate training methodologies (*see also* page 56).

Sample Power Combination Workouts

Workout for Use at Beginning of Training Year

This workout is suitable for the majority of speed development needs and combines relatively high numbers of repetitions with low loadings to develop a foundation of power. The athlete should progress to and beyond the repetitions and sets identified during the initial phases of training.

To perform the workout, alternate the weights exercise set with the plyometric one (contrast method).

Table 5.3	Power Combination Workout for Beginning of Training Year	
Weights/body weight exercise – repetitions and sets	Plyometric exercise – repetitions and sets	Recovery
Squat 3 x 12 @ 60% 1RM	Jump squat 3 x 12	0.45 sec between plyometric jumps and 90 sec between sets
Calf raises 3 x 15 @ 60% 1RM	Calf jumps 1 x 12 straight up straight down, 1 x 10 side to side, 1 x 10 straight up, straight down	Recovery as above
Single-leg squats 4 x 10 (body weight, left and right)	Hops on the spot 4 x 10 (left and right)	Athletes perform all their right-leg squats and hops first before doing so on the left leg, taking 45 sec recovery after each set
Lunge 4 x 15 holding light dumbbells	Split jumps 4 x 15	30 sec between each exercise
Bench press 4 x 20 with light dumbbells	Standing medicine ball chest pass 4 x 15	30 sec between each exercise
Crunch sit-up	Medicine ball sit-up and throw (overhead throw)	30 sec between each exercise

It is important to consider that power combination training may be less effective at conditioning speed in endurance athletes (*see* 'Interference Effect', page 130). However, the type of session set out in this table, with its emphasis on higher repetitions and shorter recoveries, should offer a reasonable physiological match. Coaches and athletes in endurance sports may find that even briefer recoveries make for greater specific conditioning benefits (as would the selection of more sport-specific exercises).

Workout for the Main Power-building Macrocycle of Training Year

This workout is suitable for sprinters, jumpers, volleyball players and basketball players, among others. This and similar types of power combination workouts should be performed in the latter stages of phase one and throughout phase two of the sport training pyramid for those involved in out-and-out speed sports, such as sprinting and high jumping (*see* page 159). In the competitive phase (phase three of the sport training pyramid) one session every 10–14 days, performed at a reduced intensity, should be enough to maintain speed and power. A similar regime would also be of benefit to martial artists in the lead-up to their competitive season. Team and field sports players should emphasise this workout pre-season.

Table 5.4	Power Combination Workout for Main Power-building Macrocycle of Training Year	
Weights/body weight exercise – repetitions and sets	Plyometric exercise – repetitions and sets	Recovery
Leg press 3 × 6 @ 80% 1RM	Double-footed jumps 3 × 6 for distance	2 min between weights sets and plyometric sets (complex methods)
Bench press 3 × 6 @ 80% 1RM	Medicine ball chest pass against wall 3 × 8	Recovery as above
Calf raises 3 × 8 @ 80% 1RM	Straight-leg jumps 3 × 8	Recovery as above
Single-leg squats 3 × 6 @ 60% 1RM	4 hops for distance from 5 stride approach	Recovery as above
Cleans 3 × 8 @ 75% 1RM	3 × 20m sprints with a 15m run-on	Recovery as above

The Sports Training Pyramid

The sports training pyramid is a basic model used for training planning (see part 8 for more detail). The apex represents the peak/competitive goal for the athlete, while the base provides the starting conditioning point. In between, various levels are constructed that emphasise a certain type/types of training. These enable the athlete to progress to a peak over a designated period.

Potentiation: a Legal Way to Boost Speed and Power Sport Performance?

Most power combination research has focused on the potentiation of training performance, but it stands to reason that if one form of dynamic exercise can prep another in the training environment, then it should also be able to do so in the competitive one.

Researchers looked at the effect of pre-squat-ting on 20m sprint performance. During the control condition, the participants performed a 20m sprint, rested for 10 minutes and then repeated the 20m sprint. During the experimental condition, the second sprint was preceded by five squat repetitions with a load equal to each participant's 5RM (the heaviest amount of weight the athlete could lift five time consecutively). Times were recorded and the results showed a mean improvement of 0.098 seconds when the second sprint was preceded by the squats. During the control condition, no improvement was observed between the first and second sprint. (Reference: *Res. Sports and Medicine*, April/June 2004; vol. 12, no. 2)

The implications of this research are potentially huge. However, before athletes and coaches get carried away, the practicalities are challenging. In reality, warming up and call-room timings for elite competitors, not to mention lugging 100kg of weights around, may preclude pre-squatting before, for example, a

100m sprint final. However, it is worth experimenting with potentiating exercises in competitions. Here are some suggestions that may be achievable. Experiment with them in training first – all should be completed five minutes before competition:

- Sprinting/jumping/throwing – perform three single-leg squats on each leg.
- Sprinting/jumping/throwing – perform five squats with a willing training partner/teammate on your back.
- Weight-lifting – perform five plyo press-ups and/or a three tuck jumps or depth jumps.

Uphill and downhill running are also forms of power training. The merits of these are covered in part 8.

PART SIX

DEVELOPING ENDURANCE

Sporting contests display the human body's capacity for endurance. A tennis player requires the stop–start endurance to last a match that could go on for more than three hours, while an elite male marathon runner needs to maintain a pace of around five minutes per mile for just over two hours to complete the 26-mile race. Ultra and adventure racers can face days, or even weeks, of endurance, for races through the Amazon rainforest and the Sahara desert (Jungle Marathon and the Marathon de Sables, respectively). In this part I provide practical information to enable coach and athlete to fully understand and condition this physical quality.

How to Imrove Endurance

To improve endurance capacity you need to:

- improve the efficiency of the heart (in particular heart rate and stroke volume);
- improve the efficiency of the vascular system and the oxygen-processing capabilities of the muscles (e.g. create more capillaries in muscles);
- improve the athlete's mental abilities and toughness;
- improve the athlete's use of fat and carbohydrate stores as fuel sources;
- improve the performance economy of the athlete;
- use meaningful testing procedures;
- follow a training plan that specifically reflects the needs of the athlete and their event/sport.

Table 6.1 (*see* pages 115–6) describes the most commonly used physical training methods to improve endurance.

Performance Economy

An endurance athlete can improve their specific performance (running, rowing, skiing and so on) by decreasing the amount of effort they put into their endurance activity from a strength, power and technique point of view. In so doing they will improve their 'performance economy'.

To give an example, a runner can boost their running economy by specifically improving leg muscle force return, joint stiffness and foot strike by plyometrics and specific running drills. This will result in the athlete becoming much more efficient – they will use less energy to run. Note: this type of training will also increase their top speed.

Building Endurance for Speed

Football and Other Field Sports

Some of the endurance training methods in Table 6.1 could also apply to developing general endurance for a football or rugby player, but they will also need to combine these with speed and agility training methods. A footballer could, for example, complete a series of 10 x 20m shuttle runs before receiving a pass and perhaps taking a shot. This will replicate the conditions found in a match when a precision skill has to be performed while fatigued.

Sprint Speed and Endurance

The faster an endurance athlete is – everything else being equal – the better endurance athlete they will be. Sprint training (*see* part 7) should not be neglected. Double-Olympic 1500m champion, Seb Coe, often trained with sprinters and utilised some of their training methods. This made him perhaps the greatest middle-distance athletes of all time (*see* page 117 for more details).

Speed Endurance and Steady State Endurance Speed

Speed endurance can be defined as the body's ability to perform an activity at a very fast speed under high anaerobic energy conditions. Examples include 800m running and tennis match play involving long rallies. It differs from steady-state endurance speed in that the training methods used to develop it are usually more short-lived and focus on the anaerobic energy system. Interval training is a key conditioner of speed endurance. Steady state endurance speed is better conditioned by efforts lasting from upward of 15 minutes at 80% of max heart rate.

Definitions of terms in the table:

Heart rate (HR) = the rate at which the heart beats consistently during a type of training

HRMax = heart rate maximum: when the heart is beating at maximum output

Base-building/long slow distance training (see page 118)

Table 6.1	Training Methods to Improve Endurance		
Method	**Workout examples**	**Key measures**	**Develops**
Base-building/duration methods, also known as long slow distance (LSD) training	Steady-paced efforts at various intensities e.g. 60 min cycle; 5 mile run; 10,000m row	HR (70–80% of HRMax) Note: For the well-conditioned endurance athlete most base-building training will be focused around 80% of HRMax Duration: Normally in excess of 30 min	Ability to sustain prolonged endurance activity. At lower heart rate levels in particular, the body will become more adept at using fat as a fuel source (see 'Fat Max', page 192). At higher levels, greater lactate/lactic acid tolerance will be developed, as will the oxygen-processing ability of muscle fibre, in particular type I slow twitch and IIa fast twitch fibres. Effort is largely sustained in the aerobic zone.
Varying pace efforts	'Controlled alternate pace' 60 min run, split as follows: Part 1: 15 min @ 70% HRMax.	HR (70–90% of HRMax) The average heart rate for the workout will be about 80% of HRMax. During the faster pace	As above. The athlete should be reminded that these serve a quality base-building purpose. Although greater speed is

Table 6.1	Training Methods to Improve Endurance cont.		
Method	**Workout examples**	**Key measures**	**Develops**
After a sufficient warm-up, the athlete simply cycles at different speeds. Efforts could last from 30 sec (near flat out) to 10 min at medium speed, perhaps on a long flat stretch of road or a hill climb.	Part 2: 1 min @ 85% HRMax, 4 min 70% HRMax recovery, repeated 6 times. Part 3: 15 min @ 70% HRMax. Uncontrolled 90 min cycle (also known as 'fartlek').	effort this may climb to near 90%, with recovery efforts being made around the 70% HRMax.	introduced, it is important to stay, on average, around 80–85% HRMax to develop optimum aerobic base condition.
Endurance specific duration based aerobic/anaerobic resistance workouts	Hill runs e.g. 10 × 3 min hill runs, with 10 min easy running between each repetition	Dependent on the number of efforts and the speed, either an aerobic or an anaerobic training effect can be elicited	Speed endurance, lactate tolerance, greater aerobic capacity, increased performance economy, increased muscle capillary growth

Sports Training Tip

Endurance athletes should not neglect weight and plyometric training. Although, as I will continue to stress, there are potential contraindications of training for endurance and power at the same time (see page 130), everything else being equal a power-trained muscle will offer greater fatigue resistance than a lesser trained one.

Athlete Profile: Seb Coe

On the importance of strength and power training for endurance athletes: 'I'm not sure that the right weight-training is done, and if I'm being harsh about it, there are some middle-distance runners in the UK who wouldn't look out of place on the front row of an elite marathon field in terms of their physiques. I'm not saying you have to look like Maurice Greene [former world 100m record holder] but you have got to be able to handle your own body weight comfortably and to develop power, and you're not going to be able to do that unless you do the right conditioning programme.'

Coe is a great advocate of free weights over fixed weights, adding: 'With machines you can isolate muscle groups very well, but there is a risk that with them you can send the rest of the body to sleep.'

Coe started out as a distance runner, winning the English schools 3000m when he was 16. He used to run cross-country, road races and long-distance track events. It was only when he was 18 that he turned his talent to the shorter middle-distance events. 'We started to focus very much on speed, which we recognised was the basis of any running . . . we realised that whatever event I did on the track I had to have speed,' explained Coe. With his coach and father, Peter, he decided to adopt this approach after watching another great British athlete, David Bedford (former 10,000m world record holder), come undone at the 1971 European Championships. Bedford did not have the basic speed to win races in terms of fast last laps and kicks, yet he was usually the fastest man in the field on paper.

Seb Coe – Career in Brief

Born: 29 September 1956
Olympic Games:
- Moscow, 1980: 1500m gold, 800m silver
- Los Angeles, 1984: 1500m gold, 800m silver
In 1979, Coe broke the 800m, 1500m and mile records within 14 days.
He is Britain's most prolific world record holder, with nine outdoor and three indoor records.

Athlete Profile: Steve Trapmore – the Importance of Base Endurance

Steve Trapmore was part of the British gold-medal-winning rowing 'eight' in the 2000 Olympics. Trapmore explained that the crew always strives to maintain high levels of aerobic fitness throughout the training year – to build a large base. More quality-orientated anaerobic pieces form part of the crew's training towards competition. The rower believes that having an extensive year-round aerobic base is crucial when it comes to maintaining consistent form across the race season.

Sports Training Tip

It has been estimated that endurance training methods that recruit fast and slow twitch muscle fibre, such as interval training, can boost intramuscular blood flow by 50–200 per cent (reference: *Acta Physiol. Scand.*, 1984 Apr; 120(4): 505–515). This crucially means more oxygen getting to the muscles to fuel aerobic energy production.

Base-building versus Sharpening/Interval Training Methods

The base-building approach to developing endurance originated in the 1960s from the work of a number of coaches, notably Australian swimming coach, Forbes Carlile, and New Zealand track coach, Arthur Lydiard. This method also goes by the name of LSD (long slow distance) training.

There is an enormous debate in the endurance training world around how much emphasis should be placed on base-building/ LSD work versus sharpening/interval training methods. I noted how an athlete like Seb Coe realised the importance of speed and power training, while another Olympic champion, rower Steve Trapmore, emphasised base-building. However, Coe could not have performed as well as he did without some form of base-building, due to the 'aerobic need' of his events. Herein lies a crucial difference between the conditioning of endurance and sprint athletes.

A sprinter will not run faster if they do not train regularly above at least 75 per cent of their maximum speed. However, an endurance athlete can expect to improve their times by training at significantly slower paces in terms of race pace, for very long periods in their training. It is even possible for an endurance athlete, such as a rower or a middle- or long-distance track runner, to reach a peak using sharpening methods in as little as eight to ten weeks, although they may have been base-building for a year or even longer.

Advocates of base-building believe that it will:

- improve the athlete's heart and lung capacity to mobilise oxygen supply to the working muscles;
- increase the oxygen-processing capability of, in particular, slow twitch muscle fibre;
- improve the athlete's ability to utilise fat as an energy source;
- increase the tolerance of muscles to sustain repeated contractions.

In turn it is argued that these changes will be more permanent in the athlete than those achieved by faster, more anaerobic-orientated training. Note: It is debatable whether training-induced changes in fibre type will ever be permanent. It has been argued that muscle fibre has a fast twitch default setting.

Athlete Profile: Peter Snell – a Product of Base-building

One of the most widely quoted exemplars for the base-building method is Peter Snell, New Zealand's triple Olympic gold medallist. Snell won 800m gold in 1960, and 800m and 1500m gold in 1964. He was coached by Arthur Lydiard, widely recognised as the father of the base-building/LSD endurance training methodology. In December 1961, Snell ran a marathon as part of Lydiard's training plan, yet two-and-a-half weeks later he ran the mile just outside four minutes. Within the next six weeks he went on to record 3:54.4 for the mile (a world record) and 1:44.3 for the 800m (another world record). This shows how speed can be born from LSD.

Double, double Olympic 5000m and 10,000m (1972 and 1976) champion, Lasse Viren from Finland, was also an exponent of the base-building method.

Sports Training Tip

When using the base-building method, the athlete should work back from when they want to be at their peak and utilise a six- to eight-week meso-cycle (period of training, see part 3) of quality sharpening training immediately before their main competition phase. Races during this later period will also bring the athlete to a peak, which they should be able to maintain for around four weeks.

Fast twitch Muscle Fibre and Endurance

As indicated in part 1, there are two basic types of fast twitch muscle fibre: type IIa and type IIb. Their importance for endurance performance has increasingly been placed under the microscope. Endurance coaches must be mindful of this research.

Type IIa

Research has indicated that these 'intermediate' fibres can, in elite endurance athletes, become as effective at producing aerobic energy as the slow twitch fibres found in non-trained subjects. Like slow twitch fibres, these fibres (and their type IIb counterparts) will benefit from an increase in capillary density, which means that more oxygenated blood (and nutrients) will be able to supply energy to the working muscles. Relevant training methods will be considered later.

Type IIb

Further research indicates that type IIb fibres (usually only associated with sprint activities) can also play a significant role in sustained energy release, to an extent probably much greater than previously thought. Specifically, researchers studied muscular enzyme changes created by endurance training and concluded that type IIb fibres were equally important as type IIa fibres to the endurance athlete in terms of their oxidative energy production and the rate of clearance of exercise-inhibiting phosphates. (Reference: *J. of App. Phys.*, 1987, 62: 438–444)

Interval training is one of the most effective ways to train fast twitch muscle fibre for endurance.

Table 6.2 displays the extent to which fibre type can be 'altered' after prolonged sport-specific training for selected endurance activities.

Table 6.2	Percentage of Slow Twitch Fibre in Deltoid (Shoulder) Muscle – Males
Endurance athlete	% slow twitch fibre in deltoid (shoulder) muscle – males
Canoeist	71
Swimmer	67
Triathlete	60

Adapted from McKardle et al., *Essentials of Exercise Physiology,* Williams and Wilkins, 1994

It is possible to achieve high levels of endurance ability with a greater anaerobic/interval-training approach, particularly for activities with a high anaerobic energy pathway requirement such as 2000m rowing (40 per cent requirement) and 1500m running (50 per cent requirement). However, it is argued that these changes will be less long-lasting. Advocates of base-building believe that the anaerobic/interval training approach will not lead to the optimum physiological conditions in an athlete to fully develop their endurance potential. In short, it is argued that the base-builder will ultimately always be a better endurance athlete than the anaerobic/faster training athlete, who places less emphasis on base-building.

Training must be Evolutionary

It is important for coach/athlete to realise that all training must be evolutionary. A marathon runner with a 10-year level of training maturity who has always employed LSD methods will be less responsive to this type of training than an athlete who has just moved up to the marathon from 5km and 10km track running. The former athlete's significant level of base endurance could now perhaps benefit from a greater emphasis on sharpening and interval training and generally increased quality in training, perhaps with more rest. It is possible that these changes may improve the marathon performance of the athlete and sustain their career.

Sports Training Tip

Doing the same type of training over and over again, although necessary to improve performance (providing it is relevant), can lead to physiological and mental stagnation/boredom. Coach and athlete must therefore be mindful of this and provide training that is stimulating in every sense of the word. Undulating periodisation (see part 8) offers the coach such a creative opportunity.

Measures of Endurance Performance

There are numerous ways to measure the training state of an endurance athlete. I have provided information on the most common, together with the pros and cons of each. It should be noted that testing is crucial if peak performance is to be achieved.

VO2max

The maximum amount of oxygen that the body can process at peak output is known as VO2max. Recently VO2max's role as an indicator of endurance performance has been devalued in favour of other measures, such as lactate threshold (although there is also a question mark over this). VO2max is measured in ml/kg of body weight per minute. Lance Armstrong, multi Tour de France-winning cyclist and ultra-endurance athlete, has a VO2max of 80–85ml/kg of body weight per minute. The untrained individual's VO2max could be less than half of this. Note: VO2max is heavily determined by genetic factors such as lung size. Specialist laboratory testing is required to determine VO2max.

Heart Rate

Measuring training intensity by heart rate (HR) and, in particular, by the use of a heart rate monitor is by far the most practical and systematic way of measuring and 'controlling' endurance training. With heart rate 'control' athletes can work in designated HR training zones, knowing that their training is developing a specific aspect of aerobic (and potentially anaerobic) fitness. Recovery, likewise, can be monitored within workouts by the use of a heart rate monitor, and away from training by the use of resting heart rate (RHR). RHR can indicate whether the athlete is in an over-trained state (*see* page 125 for more details).

Table 6.3 relates maximum heart rate to VO2max values.

Table 6.3	Heart Rate Max versus VO2max
Max HR%	VO2max
50	28
60	42
70	56
80	70
90	83
100	100

Determining Heart Rate Maximum (HRMax)

In order to plan a systematic heart rate controlled endurance programme it is necessary to know the athlete's heart rate maximum (HRMax), which will enable them to train in designated zones. HRMax tests are exhausting and should therefore not be performed when training immature athletes.

HRMax test protocols:
- Do not perform the test if the athlete is fatigued.
- Do not perform tests in close proximity to one another.
- Do not perform the test unsupervised.

Warm up with a minimum of 10 minutes' steady aerobic work (of the same type as the test) and perform some functional stretches/movements.

HRMax Controlled Test for Cyclists

Cycle for a minute at a time, increasing effort by 1km/hour each minute. Maintain a steady rate of pedalling, about 80rpm, and continue until the required pace cannot be sustained. The test will probably last between eight and twelve minutes. At the end of the test the athlete will have reached their HRMax, which should obviously be recorded.

HRMax Varies between Endurance Sports

If you are a multi-sport endurance athlete, such as a triathlete, you and your coach will need to discover sport-specific heart rate maximums. They will not be the same for running, swimming or cycling, for example.

HRMax values will be higher for running. This is because running places greater strain on the body's relevant energy systems. It should also be noted that running increases body temperature to a greater extent than swimming and cycling; more energy is required to keep the body cool, so heart rate values (and thus energy expenditure) will increase. For example, under laboratory conditions swimming HRMax is usually 13 beats slower than for running, and rowing is up to 10 beats less than for running.

Knowing a sport-specific HRMax will enable compatible HR zone training to take place across disciplines in a complementary way.

Less Controlled HRMax Test

To carry out this test, the athlete simply begins exercising at a medium to high intensity and continues to do so until they cannot carry on – again, after a suitable warm-up. At this point HRMax will be reached. This test should last between 4 and 10 minutes.

Lactate Levels and Lactate Threshold (LT)

LT threshold tests generally take the form of an incremental increase in effort against a controlled resistance, such as treadmill belt speed. Blood samples are taken, usually from the ear, for analysis of lactate accumulation, which makes this a far from practical everyday test (for more details on lactate, *see* page 5 and page 125 below).

Recent research questions the role of lactate threshold as an accurate predictor of endurance potential. It is probably far better to use measures such as time and distance tests and, in the case of more experienced performers, reflexive feedback as performance indicators.

Fat Max

For endurance athletes, the use of fat as an energy source is of crucial importance. Fat usage can significantly offset carbohydrate use and extend the athlete's range. By regularly training around 80 per cent HRMax, the athlete can significantly enhance their ability to burn fat as a fuel source. For athletes competing in events that last for more than a couple of hours, it is recommended that around 80 per cent of all training is performed in this zone. This provides further rationale for the base-building approach.

> Most of the Tour de France takes place at the base-building level, well within the fat max zone.

At exercise intensities above fat max, 2g of fat are lost for every gram of fat that could have been used at lower work ratios.

Starting an endurance race too quickly, or going too hard during the race too soon, can significantly impair endurance performance by depleting carbohydrate stores more quickly than necessary. Table 6.4 displays the total metabolic fuel use with increasing exercise intensity.

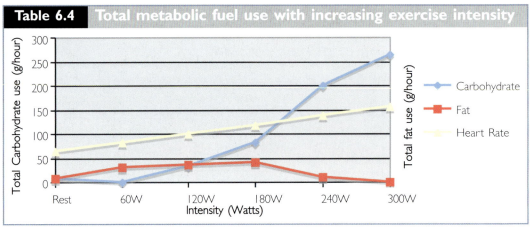

Table 6.4 Total metabolic fuel use with increasing exercise intensity

From *Peak Performance*, 224, Cycling Special

Rate of Self-perceived Exertion (RPE)

RPE (or the Borg scale) represents a subjective interpretation of exercise intensity on the part of the athlete. The scale goes from 0–20 (*see* Table 6.5). RPEs lower than 11 are not considered relevant to sports training. Please note that RPE can be applied to any type of training as long as the athlete self-rates on the basis of the activity just performed.

Table 6.5	RPE Scale
11–12	Fairly light
13–14	Somewhat hard
15–16	Hard
17–18	Very hard
19–20	Extremely hard

It may be better for the longer-endurance and ultra-endurance athlete in particular to train using heart rate control rather than RPE. Coach/athlete will then be sure that the training being performed is having a specific physiological effect and that they are well and truly within Fat Max. RPE could return a false reading. Note: research indicates that women are more likely to overestimate their RPE than men, providing potential false readings.

Athlete Profile: Paula Radcliffe – on Training

Radcliffe holds the world marathon best of 2:15.25 and has won numerous world, Commonwealth and European track and road titles. For more details on Paula Radcliffe go to: www.paularadcliffe.com.

Q: Has your training significantly evolved over the years or are the main aspects of it the same?

A: My training has progressed gradually over the years as my body has developed and been able to cope with the increased workload. There has to be a balance with mileage and quality.

Q: How many miles do you run per week in preparation for the marathon?

A: In preparation blocks for a marathon I would usually average around 140 miles per week.

Q: How do you measure the intensity of your workouts?

A: By heart rate monitor.

Q: Do you have difficulty holding yourself back in training?

A: I generally try to work as hard as I can in workouts, but I also make sure that I recover between tough days.

Q: Do you regularly test yourself in the lab or do you leave it to your road/track training session times?

A: I have a good idea from training times, but I also work with a physiologist and do lab testing.

Q: Why did you decide to run marathons and were you surprised by your success?

A: I always knew that I would progress to the marathon, but I decided to wait until I felt physically and mentally strong enough to cope with the distance. I always felt that I could move on from the marathon back to better track running. I talked to Ingrid Kristiansen [Norwegian former world-class distance and marathon runner] and she said that after she ran a marathon she ran faster on the track.

Q: How do you maintain your concentration during a race?

A: I try to concentrate on relaxing – although it sometimes doesn't look like it! On the track, because of the laps, things are a bit different, but on the roads or country the scenery and terrain are constantly changing, which helps relaxation.

Q: How do you condition yourself away from the track?

A: I also do strengthening and weights exercises designed by my physiotherapist.

Q: Do you follow a specific diet?

A: I try to eat a sensible diet and have everything in moderation. I increase my carbohydrate intake in the last few days before a marathon [carbohydrate loading is covered on page 187].

Sports Training Tip

Athletes in endurance events, particularly those lasting more than 90 minutes, should develop an in-race/training fluid replacement strategy. Research indicates that they should aim for 60g of carbohydrate per hour. This can reduce liver glycogen use by 12 per cent and muscle glycogen stores by 16 per cent, thus extending 'range'.

Altitude Training

Paula Radcliffe is an advocate of altitude training. However, the sports science jury is undecided as to whether it actually serves a positive benefit for the sea-level athlete. The rationale behind such training is that significant blood adaptations will occur when the body is subjected to a low-oxygen (hypoxic) environment. This effect will increase red blood cell count, which will permit greater quantities of oxygen to reach the working muscles. It should be noted that the athlete does not need to go to altitude or train at altitude in an attempt to accrue the purported benefits. Athletes and coaches may be familiar with hypoxic sleeping tents, which are designed to create non-training adaptations. Because of this there are numerous permutations as to the way altitude training can be carried out. These include the 'live high, train low' method and the 'live high, train high' method.

Although it is beyond the scope of this book to go into great detail about the issues surrounding altitude training, the following points should be noted:

- Research has indicated that the benefits of altitude training may be more appropriate to those whose activities have a large anaerobic (not aerobic) component. This is the result of changes that occur within the energy-creation potential of muscles, rather than increased red blood cell concentrations.
- If an endurance athlete is going to compete at altitude, then a period of four to six weeks should be allowed for acclimitisation, or they should compete (jet lag notwithstanding) the day after arrival (*see also* 'Effects of Altitude on VO2max', below).
- Altitude training may not have a significant effect on sea-level performances on return from training.

Effects of Altitude on VO2max

- VO2max will decline by 5–7 per cent per 1000m of altitude gained.
- Within 24 hours of exposure to altitude at 2200m above sea level, VO2max may fall by as much as 15 per cent.
- Under altitude conditions, VO2max will begin to increase after the initial drop but will not return to sea-level values.
- When used as determinants of training intensity, VO2max and percentage HRM values should be adjusted accordingly at altitude.

Use of Resting Heart Rate (RHR) to Determine Over-training

RHR is determined by recording the heart rate five minutes after waking. For best results this should be done over five consecutive days, with the average calculated. An increase in RHR of more than two beats could indicate that the athlete is entering an over-training state. Some endurance athletes will not train (or not train as intensely as planned) if they experience an RHR increase.

When an athlete is reaching an over-training state they will also find that their 'normal' average heart rate for a given workout increases. This is a further warning sign that should inform coach and athlete that easing back on training or a rest is needed.

Lactate and the Production of Lactic Acid

As I indicated in part 1, lactate levels increase in muscles at very low exercise intensities, as well as at much higher ones. To reiterate, lactate is not the sole consequence of anaerobic exercise. Crucially, lactate helps produce muscular energy and is created during glycolysis (*see* page 5). Glycolysis kick-starts chemical processes within muscles that produce the energy required for sustained muscular contraction.

In the untrained, lactate begins to rise as a consequence of glycolysis at around only 55 per cent VO2max. With high-intensity endurance activity the athlete achieves the 'right' conditions for acid to form in muscles. Although they will still be gulping down oxygen, it becomes insufficient to furnish enough aerobic energy. This alters the results of the chemical equations taking place in the working muscles and, instead of lactate being formed, lactic acid is produced. Specifically, lactic acid is created when pyruvic acid temporarily accepts two hydrogens (electrons).

Lactic acid, like lactate, is not a waste product. During recovery, when there is a much more plentiful supply of oxygen, lactic acid loses its two hydrogens and returns to pyruvic acid, and is used as an energy source. In fact, 50 per cent of the lactate produced during a tough workout actually goes on replenishing muscle glycogen stores during recovery. Lactic acid returns to lactate when it enters the bloodstream.

Why Lactic Acid-producing Workouts are Painful

It is believed that the pain caused by high-intensity endurance and circuit workouts results from acidic muscles aggravating nerve endings. This is also seen to 'irritate' the central nervous system, which leads to the feelings of nausea and disorientation that can result from workouts producing lactic acid.

Some athletes are better than others at tolerating the pain of tough endurance activity. As will be indicated on pages 128–9, the role of the brain in determining endurance potential is increasingly being trumpeted – literally above all else – as the key factor in determining endurance performance.

The Problems with Using Lactate Threshold as an Endurance Potential Predictor

A research team considered the use of lactate threshold (LT) as a predictor for half-marathon times. Eighteen long-distance runners performed a total of 33 half-marathons, together with an equal number of incremental field tests (4 x 2000m) to establish the relationship between running speed and blood lactate levels. During the tests the intensity of the efforts was increased in a controlled fashion. Basically, the researchers wanted to discover how fast the runners needed to run to stay within comfortable lactate levels for achieving fast half-marathon times. Speeds used in the field test ranged from 4.2 to 5.8m per second.

Following the tests, blood samples were taken and analysed. At first, it seemed that the tests were valuable predictors of half-marathon times, with test speeds corresponding to lactate concentrations of between 3.0 and 5.5mmol. These reflected the concentrations that would be expected at half-marathon race speeds. However, when the athletes actually raced, these 'strong' correlations did not really seem to matter, as 70 per cent of the athletes' final competition times fell outside the level of prediction based on the lactate levels. (Reference: *Sports Med.*, 2003; 33(1):59–73)

Coaches must therefore seriously question LT as a valuable predictor of endurance performance. Self-perceived rating and performance over selected distances in training and in races may be far better determinants of endurance potential.

Lactate Levels and Muscle Fibre

The amount of fast and slow twitch muscle fibre an athlete has will affect the amount of lactate they produce. An athlete with a higher percentage of fast twitch muscle fibre will produce greater concentrations of lactate than one with higher percentages of slow twitch muscle fibre. This can make attempts at correlating laboratory lactate tests to actual performance potentially flawed.

Interval Training

Interval training offers the endurance athlete and the speed-based/games and field athlete incredible potential. In this section I further explain the rationale for interval training and provide workout examples for sports such as tennis. (More interval workouts that target the anaerobic energy pathways for speed development are provided in part 7.)

Interval Training Structure for Endurance

The Interval For Endurance Development

This is the work/effort component. The interval can be as short as 30 seconds or as long as 20 minutes, and a workout can be designed to have a primarily aerobic or anaerobic effect.

The Recovery – Active or Passive

At the end of each interval a rest is taken. This can be active or passive.

- A **passive recovery** involves walking or standing around after the completion of each interval for a set time, or until a designated heart rate is reached. Note: the athlete should not 'flop down' and wait to perform the next interval.

- An **active recovery** is largely dependent on the endurance activity being performed; a rower could 'paddle' or a cyclist drop down to an easy rpm, between intervals. This will maintain physiological readiness for the next interval and will also increase the aerobic content of the workout, as the athlete's cardiovascular system recovers while still working.

Active recovery would generally not be used by a speed athlete, such as a sprinter, when interval training. Passive recoveries would be preferential. These would enable the athlete to emphasise the anaerobic energy pathways' adaptation towards speed, with a greater emphasis on fast twitch muscle fibre.

Endurance Training Workouts Suitable for Tennis

Efforts can be performed that reflect the stop–start nature of a tennis match and its intensity. Here are some ideas:

Base-building Workout

A base of suitable fitness could be established for tennis by performing 30-second to 2-minute intervals on a treadmill. These could be performed for an hour, with a 30-second to 3-minute recovery walk between efforts. This workout would replicate the need for a tennis player to be on their feet for long periods and, of course, the stop–start nature of match play.

The coach could control the speed of the intervals so that the player does not know exactly how intense each will be (in terms of speed and duration, given the parameters provided). This again reflects the unpredictable nature of a tennis match.

Sharpening Workout

This workout is suitable for in-season breaks or times when the player needs to re-establish more specific condition. In a gym or on a tennis court, circuit stations are designated. Each requires the player to perform a related-to-tennis skill, such as side-to-side straight-leg jumps, squat jumps, ghosted tennis shots with a racket or light dumbbell and some more general conditioning exercises, such as sit-ups or even depth jumps. The coach can control the amount of time the athlete spends on each activity, which station to run to and when to rest. The workout could also be performed on a more systematic basis, for example, completing four circuits with two minutes' recovery between circuits, on a designated repetition and exercise to exercise order. This latter option would provide the coach with greater control to develop increased condition progressively over a training period, as weekly increases in workout intensity could be planned. For example, there could be a move towards a greater number of circuits, more exercises and numbers of repetitions of each.

Lactate Stacker Interval Training

These workouts are so-called because of the very high levels of lactate (and lactic acid) they produce. They are seen to boost all measures of endurance potential (VO2max, lactate tolerance and processing ability, increased capillaries, improved performance economy and mental fortitude), all in a very short period of time.

In its purest form a lactate stacker workout requires the athlete to perform an endurance activity of up to five three-minute intervals with three minutes' (usually active) recovery between each. Each interval must be performed at a very high intensity, for example, 18 out of 20 RPE, or near/at maximum heart rate.

Consequently, the workout is very tough. The athlete needs to have a good base of training behind them before attempting it. They should also err on the side of caution and not be afraid to start with only two or three intervals. No more than two such workouts should be performed a week, and training programmes must be designed to allow optimum recovery between them. If too many are performed and not enough rest is provided, the athlete can easily enter an over-training state. They can even become depressed, as the thought of these workouts can literally overpower them and run down their nervous system.

When implemented sensibly, however, lactate stacker workouts will have a strong effect on developing the endurance (oxidative) capacity of fast twitch muscle fibre. These workouts would be suitable for the pre-competition training phase of an athlete using base-building methods.

Endurance and the Brain

As noted in part 1, muscle fibre is recruited at the behest of the brain. To this must be added the role of the mind, that more interpretive and social aspect of human mentality. When it comes to endurance success, it is often the athlete who has the most willpower, who puts up with the most discomfort, that triumphs – everything else being equal (*see* part 9, page 179 for further details on mental toughness).

Great examples are the multi-medalled rowers, Steve Redgrave and Matthew Pinsent. Their willpower was immense. They were prepared to put their bodies on the line in training and competition in order to achieve success. Consequently, more and more sports scientists are looking into the role of the brain as a determinant of endurance potential.

The Central Governor Theory

Relatively recently, research has focused on what has been called the 'central governor theory' (CGT). Tim Noakes, the famed running doctor and physiologist, has been the main driving force behind CGT. He believes there is a type of governor that resides in the brain that determines the body's ability to sustain endurance activity. This is or is not achieved by tolerating increasing intensities of exercise. He argues that its setting can be altered through the experience of intense exercise (such as lactate stacker workouts) and a corresponding shift in willpower that will permit greater endurance perseverance. This is substantiated by findings that indicate that

muscles can still hold on to 80–90 per cent of ATP and some glycogen after intense endurance efforts, when the athlete has 'decided' to stop exercising. Because of this it's theorised that the body, and its muscles in particular, will always hold on to some crucial energy-producing materials, just in case it is called upon to react in an emergency situation. This is seen to be a legacy of our unpredictable past, when our prehistoric ancestors never knew if they would need a bit more energy to run away from a sabre-toothed tiger, lurking just around the next corner, after a long day's hunting and gathering! For the endurance athlete, it means that they potentially have a reservoir of high-energy phosphates still on tap that they may be able to access, even when their body is 'saying' they do not.

It is possible that endurance athletes 'learn' how to tolerate the pain associated with lactate build-up for example, and consequently become better able to recruit their muscle fibres.

The Central Fatigue Hypothesis

Closely related to the above thoughts on the CGT is another self-preservation consideration, which is again apt when thinking of the sabre-toothed tiger. Noakes has also explored this endurance determinant. Although this functions in a different protective realm, it can have an equally significant influence on muscle fibre recruitment. The 'central (nervous system) fatigue hypothesis' (CFH) postulates that the brain will 'shut down' the body under certain conditions, when there is a perceived threat to damage to vital organs, irrespective of how 'fit' an individual's endurance system is. The conditions specifically identified are high altitude and high temperatures.

However, researchers believe that the CFH could also apply under less taxing external conditions. As Noakes writes: '. . . there is no evidence that exhaustion under these conditions is associated with either skeletal muscle "anaerbosis" or energy depletion . . . There is sufficient evidence to suggest that a reduced central nervous system recruitment of the active muscles terminates maximum exercise.'

Basically, Noakes is arguing that endurance athletes again can still have more in the tank, and that tricking or working on mental strategies to unleash it could well be the most significant aspect of training for the mature endurance athlete (*see* below). (Reference: Peak Performance Keynote Lecture, 1 September 2000, 'Physiological models to understand exercise fatigue and the adaptations that predict or enhance athletic performance')

Tricking the Brain to Achieve Greater Endurance Performance

Pre-cooling

Various methods have been employed to try to 'trick' the brain into not shutting down muscle fibre recruitment under extreme conditions. Most of these centre on pre-cooling strategies to the body, notably to the brain. Contemporary endurance athletes often pre-cool their bodies so that it takes longer for them under race conditions to heat up to levels that could have a negative effect on performance. Cyclists have experimented, for example, with types of ice helmets, which by cooling the brain seem to be able to trick the body into releasing increased endurance tolerance.

It has, however, been argued that pre-cooling strategies are more likely to benefit those in activities lasting half an hour or less. This is because after this time, skin and body temperature equalise between athletes who have been subject to pre-cooling and those who have not.

Coach and athlete should systematically experiment with these methods in training, before using them competitively.

Avoiding Over-training Syndrome (OTS)

Resting heart rate (*see* page 125) has been identified as a means to assess whether an athlete is reaching an over-training state. Other signs include restlessness, inability to sleep, irritability, greater susceptibility to infections, aching muscles and difficulty concentrating. Athlete and coach should continually be on the lookout for any of these symptoms. Failure to prevent the early stages of over-training, known as over-reaching, may lead to injury and more permanent illness.

Endurance athletes are much more likely to suffer from over-reaching and over-training than power/speed athletes, due to the consistency and the nature of the strain placed on their bodies. Endurance athlete and coach should:

- schedule in ample rest days and periods in the training plan;
- vary training over easy, medium and hard microcycles and mesocycles (training periods);
- evaluate workouts and adapt training accordingly. (I have provided a guide to workout monitoring in Table 6.6 below. This information should be discussed between coach and athlete and recorded in a training diary. *See also* part 9 for objective ways to monitor training and competition.)

Table 6.6	Workout Rating Guide for Athlete and Coach

Guidance criteria

1 Not a good workout, virtual non-attainment of workout goal

2 Disappointing, partial completion of workout target

3 Average workout, athlete did not maintain the quality desired, perhaps on the last repetitions or part of the run or cycle, although the main goals were accomplished sufficiently

4 Good workout – achieved all targets

5 Excellent workout – surpassed workout goals and felt great

The athlete should record the rating in their training diary and provide objective feedback as to the results. The coach should be involved in this process and all comment must be as objective as possible. Note: The process of workout rating requires effective goal-setting and evaluation (*see* parts 8 and 9).

Training for Endurance and Weight-training – the Interference Effect

Nearly all endurance athletes weight-train. For weight-training to directly improve any sporting ability, the strength gained in the weights room has to be channelled into the activity. This channelling process (*see* page 56) relies on selecting exercises that reflect the movement patterns of the sport in question, and incorporating them into a relevant training programme. However, even when this process is followed correctly, the direct contribution of weight-training to improving endurance has often been found

to be minimal. This is largely a consequence of what is known as the 'interference effect'.

The interference effect dictates that when muscle fibre – particularly the fast twitch variety – is trained by two distinct and non-complementary training methods, such as weight-training and intense interval training, conflicting physiological results occur. It is almost as if one training method cancels out the other. The key question is: how can fast twitch fibre (in particular type IIa) be expected to take on a greater power-producing function through weight-training when it is being targeted in the same training plan – even the same workout – by high-intensity interval training designed to develop endurance? A similar argument can be forwarded for the conflict between slow twitch and fast twitch fibre response under the same training conditions.

Evidence of the interference effect has come from numerous surveys. As an example, a team of researchers looked at the effects of three different weight-training programmes on 18 university rowers during their winter training. One group performed 18–22 high-velocity, low-resistance repetitions, while another did six to eight low-velocity, high-resistance repetitions and a third did no weight-training at all. All weight-training exercises were rowing-specific and were performed four times a week for five weeks, while the subjects continued with their normal endurance rowing training.

The results? When the rowers were tested on a rowing machine, no difference was found between any of the groups in terms of rowing power. This led the research team to conclude that once an athlete reaches a good level of proficiency in a sport (become training mature), weight-training is less likely to directly improve performance. (Reference: *Journal of Sports Sciences*, 1989; 7: 205–214)

Other, similar findings have been made by research teams across other sports, such as swimming and running. I have personally heard similar comments from endurance athletes, especially those with high levels of training maturity, for example, Barcelona gold medal rower Jonny Searle (*see* comments of Grant Hackett, below).

Athlete Profile: Grant Hackett – On Weight-Training

Like many endurance athletes and the sports science world, Hackett – Australia's double Olympic 1500m freestyle gold medal winner – was slightly unsure about whether weight-training had really benefited, in particular, his longer-distance swimming. 'You get the endurance from the pool so the weights are mainly about power. It's hard to put it quantifiably but I feel that they have definitely helped my sprint swimming and perhaps to a degree the 1500m.'

Beating the Interference Effect

Here is one of the few relevant running-based studies that indicates that weight-training can directly improve endurance performance. Exercise physiologist Ron Johnston found improvements in running economy after a 10-week weight-training programme. In this study, 12 trained female distance runners were split into two groups. All the athletes ran at least 20 miles a week. One group weight-trained and ran, and the other group just ran. The weight-training athletes trained three times a week; their workouts consisted of 14 exercises involving the upper body, abdominal muscles and legs.

It was discovered that the weights and running group improved their upper body strength by 24 per cent and leg strength by 34 per cent. Lactate tolerance (as measured by lactate threshold) and VO2max did not change in either group. However, the weight-training runners' running economy improved significantly from 3.8 per cent to 4.5 per cent at the three running speeds used in the study – basically they had to put in less effort to cover their distances than runners in the other group. It is estimated that such an improvement in economy could knock a couple of minutes off a 5000m time.

However, to sound a note of caution, the runners in this study were relatively inexperienced weight-trainers and so were more likely to respond positively to the training. Had they been seasoned campaigners, the results could have been different. Numerous other research studies suggest that immature athletes (with respect to endurance and weight-training) are much more likely to benefit from weight-training than experienced athletes. (Reference: *European Journal of Applied Physiology*, 1991; 62: 251–255)

In the light of these research findings, the coach must carefully consider the training maturity and needs of the athlete, specifically when putting together a weight-training programme. It is very unlikely that weight-training per se will improve endurance performance directly. However, when combined with plyometrics and hill running, for example, the chances of it being successful are much greater. Nor should weight-training's benefits for pre-conditioning and injury prevention be neglected (*see* part 2).

Endurance Athletes Still Need to Weight-train

Despite the interference effect, endurance athletes should not neglect weight-training for pre-conditioning purposes (see part 2) as it will, for example, strengthen soft tissue, even if direct performance gains (particularly for mature athletes) are potentially minimal.

Beating the Interference Effect with Specific Resistance Training Methods

Some resistance and weight-training methods are less likely than others to create an interference effect. Here are some examples:

Circuit Training (CT), Circuit Resistance Training (CRT) and Aerobic Circuit Training (ACT)

These offer a close physiological match to mainstay endurance training, such as cycling, running or rowing, using short recoveries, high numbers of repetitions and constantly elevated heart rates.

CT uses body-weight exercises; CRT uses weights exercises with light-to-medium weight loads; and ACT combines body-weight and weight exercises with a significant aerobic element, for example, six minutes of running at the end of each circuit.

All these types of workout, particularly the latter, have been shown to improve strength, lactate tolerance and VO2max. The oxygen-processing and power capacity of slow twitch muscle fibre is improved, while fast twitch fibre is developed in a way that has synergy with anaerobic endurance conditioning, thus minimising the interference effect. (An example of a rowing-specific circuit is provided on pages 80–3.)

PART **SEVEN**

DEVELOPING SPEED AND AGILITY

The search for more speed is perhaps the Holy Grail of sports performance. At all levels it is a truism that, everything else being equal, the faster, more agile athlete will be the better player/winner. This part breaks down speed into different 'speed types' and shows athlete/coach how to develop this most precious of sporting commodities. It provides speed-training drills, workouts, exercises and practices for sprinters, jumpers, footballers, basketball players and other court and field sport athletes.

The importance and rationale for improving speed for endurance athletes is also considered.

Speed Types

The speed required for sport comes in various forms. It can be applied in a straight line, over a turn or other rotational movement, through a punch, hit, kick, tackle, throw, jump, dive or reaction. It may involve the whole body, as in sprinting, or be unleashed ultimately through a limb, as with the javelin throw or tennis serve. Given these variations, it is helpful to define specific 'speed types'. This will enable athlete/coach to understand just what type of speed (or combination of speeds) is required for their particular sport and, crucially, how it can best be conditioned.

Optimum Speed

Too much speed can be a disadvantage, although this may not be apparent initially. If a long jumper, for example, builds up too much speed on the runway, they may not be able to take off into an effective jump. This is because they will have too little time on the take-off board to generate the force needed to convert speed into distance.

Similar problems occur in many other sports. In rugby union, Jonny Wilkinson knows his range when it comes to place kicks. He has developed his rhythm with painstaking practice over many years, and inevitably slots the ball between the posts. The England and Lions half-back *could* swing his boot faster at the ball in an attempt to gain additional metres, but would probably sacrifice accuracy as a result. It is therefore important for athletes to determine with their coaches an appropriate speed for their particular sport's skills that does not compromise technical execution.

Out-and-out (Sprint) Speed

Some sports activities demand maximum expression of speed, sprinting being the most obvious example. However, it is important to note that, while the sprint athlete must move their limbs as fast as possible during the race, they must do this in a relaxed manner, since the effort involved in 'trying too hard' will tighten muscles and slow performance. Out-and-out speed therefore calls for mastery of technique, plus the ability to relax while the body is operating at maximum intensity (while at the same time recruiting the largest, most powerful amounts of fast twitch muscle fibre). (*See* page 142 for a 'key tips' guide to achieving optimum sprinting technique, and page 143 for out-and-out speed practices.)

These times display just how fast the body must react to develop speed:

Table 7.1	Ground Contact Times and Selected Sports	
Sport		Ground contact time (sec)
Sprinting		.090
Bounding		.175
Long jump take-off		.110
High jump take-off		.130
Hop		.180
Depth jump 40cm drop		.200
Depth jump 100 cm drop		.300
Marathon		<.400

Adapted from G. Dintimen and B. Ward, *Sports Speed*, Human Kinetics, 2003

Acceleration Speed

In order to achieve out-and-out and/or other speed types, a period of acceleration is usually required. A sprinter, for example, must leave their blocks from a stationary 'set' position; a footballer will need to turn and sprint to get on to the end of a pass from an equally static or off-balance position; while a tennis player must deliver their serve from a stationary base. Developing this accelerative ability calls for different training methods and practices.

Developing Acceleration Speed

Acceleration is all about overcoming resistance – the ground, an opponent or an object – as fast as possible. The speed ability will also rely on reaction speed, the ability to read a match situation (where appropriate), specific sports skill and other relevant conditioning methods. I have provided two acceleration workouts below (most of the exercises described can be found in more detail elsewhere in this book).

Table 7.2	Acceleration Workout for Sprint Athletes (could also be used for conditioning acceleration speed for field and racket sports players)

Pre-workout warm-up: 5–10 minutes of jogging and specific warm-up exercises

Exercise	Repetitions	Comments/technique tips
Speed bounds	4 × 20m with full recovery	Concentrate on pushing the ground backwards
Sprint starts	4 × 20m with full recovery	Perform at 90% effort, translating the speed bound driving movement to the acceleration needed to get away from the stationary sprint start. The athlete should stay low to aid acceleration.
Start from press-up position	6 × 10m	Concentrate on a dynamic move from the floor, driving the arms as powerfully as possible

Football and rugby players require dynamic multi-directional acceleration. This is crucial over comparatively short distances, as a break by a rugby player, for example, can breach the defence and open up the game in just 5 to 10 metres. The drills described in Table 7.2 are more suited to developing a base of acceleration speed, which can then be enhanced by the more specific drills that follow.

Table 7.3	Acceleration Workout for Rugby and Football Players

Pre-workout warm-up: 5–10 minutes of jogging and specific exercises

Exercise	Guidance	Repetitions	Comments
Sideways turn and 10m sprint	Stand sideways on to the direction of acceleration, turn and 'drive' the legs back to accelerate as fast as possible over 10m. As with the sprinter, a low driving position will assist acceleration.	10 in both directions with 1 min recovery	The drill can be made more specific – e.g. a rugby player could carry a ball
Two player spin and sprint in same direction	Two players stand shoulder to shoulder, 1m apart. On a command, they turn away from each other to run in the same direction towards a ball or cone	10, practising turns to the left and right	A low body position and driving arm action is crucial to maximising acceleration. The players must also be aware of their proximity to one another.
Various ladder foot speed drills (see page 146)	Take low steps and concentrate on foot ground contact	20–30 with incomplete and varied recovery to simulate match fatigue	Practise running through the ladder, forwards, backwards and sideways

Endurance Speed

Speed training is often neglected by endurance athletes, such as marathon runners and triathletes, yet speed is crucial to their success. The faster an endurance athlete is:

- the easier it will be to cruise at slower speeds during training and competition;
- the more power is available for hill climbs;
- the more power is available for surging during a race to burn off the opposition;
- the more they will have in reserve for a killer sprint finish.

For the purposes of this book, I will define endurance speed as 'the ability to sustain repeated powerful and fast muscular contractions over predominantly aerobic race and training conditions, for as long as possible'. Examples of endurance speed workouts can be found in part 6.

Speed Endurance

I define speed endurance for the purposes of this book as the ability of the body to perform an activity at a very fast speed under conditions where a high level of anaerobic energy production is required. It differs from endurance speed in that the training methods used to develop it are usually more short-lived and focus on the anaerobic energy system.

How to Develop Speed Endurance – Sample Workouts

1. Quality Out-and-out Short-speed Endurance Interval Training

For: 100m sprinters, long and triple jumpers, field and racket sports players
Develops: the immediate anaerobic pathway
Speed of runs: 100 per cent
Workout: 40/60/80/60/40 sprints, with three minutes' recovery between each
Note: This workout will also have a secondary effect on developing the short-term anaerobic energy system.

2. Quality Out-and-out Longer-speed Endurance Workout

For: 100/200m sprinters and rugby wingers
Workout: 2 x 2 x 120m sprints, with six minutes between runs and 10 minutes between sets
Speed of runs: 100 per cent using a rolling start
Develops: more enduring speed endurance, in comparison to the first workout
Note: Requires a good prior level of conditioning before it can be performed optimally and without injury risk. The use of preparatory speed endurance interval training for a macrocycle (*see* part 8) is a must. The limit for 100-per-cent effort running is about 120m. This type of workout will increase the athlete's ability to hold on to top speed for longer as it targets the immediate and, in particular, the short-term anaerobic pathway.

3. Speed Endurance Workout with Increased Endurance Emphasis

For: football midfielders and 400m runners
Workout: 200/250/300m runs x 2, with four minutes between runs and six minutes between sets
Speed of runs: 90 per cent of maximum
Develops: the short-term anaerobic system and creates high levels of lactate (more so than workout 2, everything else being equal). It is designed to improve an athlete's lactate tolerance.
Note: This workout would suit a footballer in the early stages of conditioning. However, more specific practices must be developed as the season approaches and in-season. A 400m athlete could normally use this type of workout in the pre-competition macrocycle training phase.

Response Speed

In many sports, a skill has to be performed in response to a cue. This cue could be aural, as with a sprinter reacting to the starting gun, or visual, as with a boxer avoiding a punch, a footballer responding to a change in the opposing team's formation, or a cricket batsman reacting to the ball.

Factors that Affect Response Speed

There are a multitude of factors that affect response speed. These include:

- **strength and power:** to overcome inertia, an opponent, or an object when reacting;
- **visual acuity:** the ability to 'see' where a gap is and get through it, as is the case in rugby, for example;
- **neural response:** the ability to be sufficiently motivated and focused to get the body to react as fast and effectively as possible (see part 9).

Selected examples of response speed practices can be found on pages 147–8.

Leaving No Stone Unturned – Speed Practices

Clive Woodward was known for leaving no stone unturned when he coached England to victory in the 2001 rugby World Cup. Among the numerous conditioning and motivational methods used were specific agility training and visual acuity training. The latter would be performed with the use of computers, and was not that dissimilar to the type of tests used by opticians to determine field of vision.

Body Part Speed

For some sports a particular limb must move as fast as possible. This might be in order to throw an implement as far as possible, as is required in the javelin. Occasionally it might be to throw as fast as possible, as with a baseball pitch. Although this speed and power will be generated through the athlete's body, the throwing arm is the crucial link in the speed chain. It is this limb that will advance the implement/ball to optimum velocity at the point of release. If the arm is not fast (and strong) enough to do this then performance will obviously suffer.

Sports Training Tip

Although body part speed is worthy of isolation in terms of specific drills and practices, it should always be rooted in whole-body speed training. This is because, in most cases, this speed type will be manifested through the interaction of numerous other body parts. For example, the javelin thrower will need a strong torso to enable the full force of their arm to contribute to the javelin release through the delivery strides and the point of release.

Team Speed

The need for team speed is obvious in the case of a sprint relay team. However, it is crucial to the success of virtually all other team sports, where players must move quickly and in concert with one another to score a try or defend as a unit, as in rugby. Developing this shared speed should be a training requirement in team sports. As we will see in part 8, however, maintaining the speed (and condition) of individual players in a team can be difficult, particularly over a long season with numerous matches.

To develop team speed, the coach must develop practices that allow their team to be as quick and effective a unit as possible. A basketball full court press is an example of a team speed requirement (one that also relies on supreme specific endurance conditioning). Training drills must therefore tax the energy systems of the players in a way that matches game situations.

Sports Training Tip

It would be remiss of the team coach to train all the players in the same way. Specific programmes need to be implemented for individuals, yet these must at all times dovetail with the needs of the team. In doing so, speed (or any other conditioning element) will be optimised for the player and the team.

Over-speed

The term 'over-speed' is used to describe training efforts that allow the athlete to perform a speed skill to a speed beyond what is normally achievable. It can involve the use of specialist equipment such as elastic cords, which literally drag the athlete to higher velocities, or lower-tech (but equally effective) methods such as downhill sprinting and throwing lighter implements or balls than those used in competition. Over-speed training is covered in detail on pages 151–3.

Agility Speed

Agility is another key sports speed requirement. It is characterised by quick feet and hands, body co-ordination and fast reactions. Its execution depends on a mixture of balance, out-and-out speed, response speed, acceleration speed, strength, flexibility and co-ordination. Although an athlete's agility also relies heavily on the possession of optimum sports technique and 'match sense', it can be enhanced by specific agility speed conditioning methods (*see* pages 149–51).

Rotational Speed

Rotational speed is a key speed requirement in many sports. Footballers rotate their bodies to turn and chase down opponents or the ball, while tennis players have to 'wind' up their body to hit a serve, a baseline forehand or backhand pass. In track and field sports, discus throwers spin with almost balletic grace before releasing their implements with the incredible force needed to achieve huge distances. Rotational speed can be vastly improved by the use of appropriate drills and training methods (*see* pages 146–8).

Sports Training Tip

Speed training should be a regular feature of *all* athletes' conditioning programmes, even endurance athletes. Everything else being equal, the faster athlete will be the best athlete.

Sports Training Tip

Pre-conditioning is a must for the speed athlete (see part 2). Speed activities place great strain on the body, so the athlete's 'structure' must be as prepared as possible to withstand these forces.

Running Technique

Running speed is obviously a key feature of many sports. In this and previous parts I have provided numerous ways to 'condition' this attribute through the use of specific training, such as plyometric and power combination training. However, these techniques will not allow for the full expression of, especially, out-and-out sprint speed unless the mechanics of the running action or sports skills are optimally mastered. This section covers the technical basics of the sprint running action and considers the adjustments required to the running action for field and racket sport players.

Leg Speed

An elite male sprinter will be able to achieve a stride rate of 4.5 to 5 strides per second.

Athlete Profile: Jason Gardener, World and European indoor 60m champion and Olympic 4 x 100m gold medallist – on Sprint Form Detail

Gardener does hundreds of sprint drills during his training to cement perfect sprinting technique (including many of the exercises described in parts 2 and 3). Says Gardener 'My technique is not too bad from the side, but from the front it's got some problems. There's a lot of rotation going on [wasteful side-to-side movements that reduce the amount of power Gardener places on the track]. I think it's because of the way I'm built – my hip position and my running gait. I'm not massively bow-legged, but I've one leg that is more externally rotated, and if I don't keep on top if it, it affects my position when I'm running.'

Sprinting epitomises out-and-out speed in sport. Top-class male sprinters reach speeds approaching 30mph. To move this fast they are in possession of a neuromuscular system that enables them to put as much power down on to the track in as short a time as possible (*see* Table 7.1), while moving their limbs as fast as possible. As I stress, they must do this in as relaxed a state as possible.

Key Technical Aspects of Sprinting Technique

1 Relaxed neck and facial muscles.
2 High knee pick-up, with thighs lifting to a position parallel to the ground, knees driving forwards, not up and down.
3 Full drive of the leg behind the body – pushing the body forwards.
4 Heel coming up close to buttocks during the pull-through (return) phase.
5 Upright torso.
6 Arms moving backwards and forwards in a powerful but relaxed manner, in harmony with legs. Shoulders kept square to the front and a 90-degree angle at the elbow joint maintained for the majority of the arm swing.
7 Each foot striking the ground in front of the body (but not so far as to lead to braking).
8 'Pulling/clawing' of the track (or running surface) back towards the body with the foot.
9 Foot striking the ground from a toe-up position, but with the power coming from the balls of the feet (a toe-down position will inevitably lead to a loss of power as the ankle collapses under the force it is subject to before propelling the sprinter forwards). Note: there will be some heel contact.

Improvements in sprinting are attributable to:

- an increase in stride frequency (leg speed)
- an increase in stride length
- the ability to relax
- technical proficiency
- an increase in muscular power
- a progressive training plan

Developing Out-and-out Speed Practices

For the following practices, I have provided some key words for coaches to use for these workouts so that they can 'sow' into the mind of their athletes just what is required of the session. The power of suggestion is a key aspect for developing the mental contribution to all sports training. (*See* part 9.)

Acceleration runs: Over a distance of 60m, the athlete gradually builds up their speed so that by the 40–50m mark they are at full speed. The drill should be performed individually as competition can produce tension. Key descriptive word for the coach to use during the session: 'smooth'.

Build-up/'flying' runs: These require the athlete to build up to a relatively short period of flat-out running. They are more intense than acceleration runs in that the emphasis is placed on leg speed during the flat-out portion – the athlete attempts to move their legs as fast as possible. An example of this type of run would be a 30m acceleration period followed by 15m flat-out. Key descriptive word for the coach to use during the session: 'leg speed' or 'turnover'.

Fast/coast/fast 60m runs with 15m run-on: The 60m is divided into three 20m sections. The athlete begins 15m before the first 20m and accelerates to sprint the first near flat-out. For the second 20m, they relax very slightly, and then kick again to sprint flat-out for the third 20m. The third 20m will often prove difficult as the athlete will be trying to build greater speed from an already fast base, but if mastered,

it will increase the athlete's out-and-out speed. Key descriptive words for the coach: 'more speed, followed by more speed'.

Speed bounding into sprinting: The athlete performs speed bounds over 15m and then progresses over a number of strides to the sprint action, to continue sprinting for a further 30m. The athlete strives to maintain the deliberate 'drive' of the speed bound more subtly into the sprint action. Key descriptive word for the coach to use: 'drive'.

Over-speed methods for increasing out and out sprint speed are covered on pages 151–3.

Mastering Technique

Technical proficiency is crucial for developing out-and-out speed. Performing technical drills, such as sprint drills for a sprinter, will be beneficial in this respect. A drill usually takes an aspect of the main sport's technique and breaks it down so that it is worked on in isolation. The high-knee sprint drill is a case in point for the sprinter.

However, too much emphasis on drills can be a problem. This shows just how difficult it can be to achieve peak sporting performance. For example, too great an emphasis on the high-knee drill could result in an up-and-down running action, as the drive phase of the sprint action would be neglected. The neuromuscular system would pattern a movement that would ultimately be detrimental to sprinting. It is therefore crucial that coach and athlete are fully aware of what they are doing in their training at all times. In this respect, training planning and evaluation become crucial, as is of course selection and use of the most relevant exercises and drills for a particular athlete and their sport.

Running and Other Sports

The sprint running action has to be modified to account for the nature of other sports. Great football strikers, like Thierry Henry and Ronaldo, possess not only great speed but also the agility and rotational body power required to twist and turn while running and keeping the ball under control.

In such sports, the sprinting action has to be modified; as there are very few occasions when a 'pure' out-and-out sprint can be made. Even if a rugby player makes a 40–50m sprint to the try line, he will still have to carry the ball under one arm. He may also have to cope with running on soft ground, while angling the run towards the posts. Similarly, a tennis player will often 'scamper' rather than sprint to the net to retrieve a drop shot and will keep their centre of gravity low as they strive to reach these and other returns. In consequence, speed training must be designed to replicate these specific sports running skills.

There has been some research on the modified sprint action required for various racket and field sports, with mixed results. Carrying a rugby ball under one arm, for example, has not surprisingly been found to increase sprint speed in comparison with two-handed carrying. Additionally, it has been discovered that field sports players tend to use a more flat-footed running action.

Does Straight-line Speed Make for a More Agile and Speedier Runner?

It is often assumed that athletes who are fast when travelling in a straight line will be fast in any direction. Young and associates researched the impact of straight-line speed training on rotational/change of direction speed, and vice versa. Thirty-six males were tested on a 30m straight sprint and six change-of-direction tests; the latter involved two to five changes of direction sprints at various angles. These tests took place before and after a six-week training period. Two groups were established:

- Group 1 performed 20–40m straight-line sprints.
- Group 2 performed 20–40m, 100-degree-angle, change of direction sprints.

Not surprisingly, group 1 improved their straight-line sprinting performance. However, this increased zip did not translate into speedier turns. In fact, the researchers discovered that the more complex the change of direction/turning task, the less transference there was from the straight-line speed training. Again not to much surprise, the turning/change of direction training gave a major boost to group 2's performances on the turn and sprint test, but had no impact on straight-line speed. (Reference: *Sports Med.*, 1997, Sep; 24(3): 147–56)

These findings have important implications for athletes and coaches in sports like football and tennis where players have to turn constantly. It seems that the ability to rotate the body at speed is a highly specific skill that requires specialist conditioning.

Foot Strike Variation

To maximise speed and power delivery, athlete and coach should carefully analyse the foot strike variations required of their sport, and condition these through the use of appropriate drills.

Kovacs and associates looked at the relevance of foot positioning, particularly foot-landing positions when athletes performed depth jumps. Specifically, the researchers addressed the force generated from flat-footed versus forefoot ground contacts. Ten healthy male university students performed two types of depth jump from a 0.4m high box placed 1.0m from the centre of a force plate. They were instructed to land either on the balls of their feet, without the heels touching the ground during the subsequent jump, or to land on their heels. Three successfully performed trials per jump of each type were included in the analysis. The researchers discovered that the first and second peak in force generation, as determined from the vertical force-time curves, were 3.4 times greater and 1.4 times lower for flat-footed landing as opposed to forefoot landings. (Reference: *Med. Sci. Sports Exerc.*, 1999 May; 31(5): 708–16)

These findings have crucial implications for optimum speed, agility and power conditioning. Even though a flat-footed landing depth jump will develop power, this may not channel optimally into enhancing the agility and power of a player in a specific sport. To give some examples: a sprinter could prosper more from forefoot landing depth jumps as the sprint action is performed from a similar foot-strike position, whereas a basketball or volleyball player may develop greater vertical spring – a key requirement of their games – by using flat-footed landing depth jumps. Muscle firing patterns are very specific, and an off-key response could result if the conditioning drill does not mirror the sport skill.

The Impact of Footwear on Speed Performance

Space precludes an in-depth analysis of specialist sprint and speed training shoes; however, it is important to understand that the shoes worn by the athlete can significantly affect their performance, regardless of sport.

Selecting the Right Shoes

Track and field spikes designed for out-and-out speed have very little heel support, as the heel hardly impacts the ground during the acceleration and optimum speed phases of sprint races from 10–400m. They are designed to 'push' the athlete's weight forwards and are obviously very light. Technological innovations include hiding the laces behind zips in order to reduce drag as the foot is pulled through the air. Some researchers indicate that this can save 0.05 seconds over 100m.

Speed training shoes also exist that are a hybrid between training shoes and sprint spikes. These can be a very useful addition to the training kit of many sportspeople, since they provide more cushioning and greater support than spikes and are therefore easier on the joints. However, they will slightly compromise the ability to generate optimum speed when compared to spikes, due to their greater cushioning (absorbent) properties.

Funds permitting, athletes should experiment with different styles of sprint spikes, as one type may suit them better than others. Research has suggested that a shoe's 'bend stiffness' can improve or impair sprint performance. Sport scientists from the University of Calgary in Canada discovered that stiffer shoes increased sprint performance over 40m sprint trials (Reference: *Sports Biomech.*, 2004 Jan; 3(1): 55–66)

Football, rugby and hockey boots and tennis shoes are becoming as high-tech as sprint spikes. It is now possible to have lightweight football boots, for example, designed on the last of sprint spikes, which are often worn by forwards. It should be noted that they offer less support and protection than more traditional boots. As with discovering the right spike for sprinters, other athletes should experiment in training to discover which variant of their playing footwear optimises their performance. Note: Field sport athletes may well have two or even three different choices of footwear to suit different playing conditions.

Coach/athlete must carefully scrutinise the

shoes (and other kit) needed to optimise performance, but the choice must be made on the basis of what enhances performance for the athlete – 'fashion' should not *just* be followed.

Developing Rotational Speed/agility Speed

The workout ideas that follow can be used by field and racket sports players and martial artists, among others, to develop a foundation of specific rotational and agility speed and power. The exercises can be combined into a single workout or used as elements of a sport-specific warm-up.

Warm up with 5–10 minutes of jogging. Floor speed/agility ladders can be purchased through specialist sports retailers,* although you can easily make your own by taping lines or using chalk to mark rungs on a suitable floor. Ladders usually have 20 rungs, spaced approximately 35cm apart.

| Exercise 7.1 | **Floor Speed/agility Ladder Drills** |

1 Run through the ladder, one foot in each rung at a time, gradually increasing speed with each repetition. Drive the arms backwards and forwards to aid speed.
2 Run through the ladder backwards, one foot in each rung at a time.
3 Skip sideways through the ladder, one foot in each rung at a time. To perform this drill, the athlete should drop their buttocks towards the ground, keep their arms outstretched in line with their shoulders and remain 'light' on their forefeet.
4 Diagonal bounce: stand facing the ladder and perform a two-footed, straight-leg jump into

*To purchase floor speed/agility ladders contact http://www.sports-fitness.co.uk.
See also SAQ International (page 150).

the first rung, then spring diagonally to the right, just outside the foot ladder and in line with the second rung. Then, from the two-footed landing position, spring diagonally back into the third rung, then spring diagonally to the left, opposite the fourth rung, and back into the fifth. Complete the floor ladder length in this manner.

Note: There are endless permutations of floor ladder drills. Ladders can, for example, be placed into L-shapes or side by side. Sport skills can be performed with them, such as a catch and pass for rugby.

Technique Tip

When agility training, coach and athlete must ensure that ground contacts are light and fast.

Exercise 7.2 Turn and Sprint Drill

The athlete stands with their back to their coach. To a command, they turn and sprint 10m. Do five repetitions turning to the right and five to the left.

Technique Tip

The athlete should keep their body low as they rotate, and their initial strides short. Acceleration is boosted by pumping the legs back from the hip to 'drive' the ground backwards.

Exercise 7.3 Compass Run

Using five cones (or suitable markers), place one in the centre of the 'compass' and the others 5m away from it at the compass points. The athlete starts from the centre cone and runs and touches each compass point cone. They should always return to the centre cone before setting off for the next one. Efforts can be timed. Do three repetitions, with four minutes' recovery between each.

As a variation: run backwards to each compass point, stopping in line with each cone and sprinting (forwards) back to the central cone before adjusting position and running backwards in turn to the next compass point.

The drill should be performed with control in the early stages while the athlete develops confidence and skill, as the turn and the change from backwards to forwards running can be very demanding.

Medicine Ball Drills

- **Medicine ball throw with rotation:** The athlete starts with their feet just beyond shoulder-width apart, holding a medicine ball with their hands placed on the sides of the ball. They should bend their knees and rotate to the right, and swing the ball well beyond their right hip. The ball is then swung past the hip while being lifted. The athlete should perform a few more preliminary swings before throwing the ball as far as they can. Lifting through the legs and rotating through the hips will add distance to the throw. Do 10 repetitions to the right and 10 to the left. Take 30 seconds' recovery between throws and one minute between left and right sets. Distances can be measured to monitor improvement.
- **Medicine ball run, pick-up and throw:** A partner is needed for this drill. Place two cones 10m apart and a medicine ball by the furthest one. The athlete runs to the cone, picks up the medicine ball and, in one movement, throws the ball with a chest pass action to their partner. They then turn and run back to the first cone, touch it, turn and run back to the second cone to pick up and throw the (now replaced) medicine ball again. Do two sets of five repetitions with five minutes' recovery.

Further medicine ball drills are found on pages 101–2.

Floor Ladder Speed

A player's speed through a floor ladder can indicate much about their quickness. Times of less than 2.8 seconds and 3.4 seconds through a 20-rung ladder, one foot in each rung at a time, for example, are regarded as 'excellent' for college males and female athletes respectively. (Reference: SportsCoach at wwwbrimac.demon.co.uk)

Using Other Speed and Agility Equipment

The coach/athlete has a variety of speed and agility enhancing equipment available to them. It is beyond the scope of this book to go into detail, but coach/athlete should consider the use of small hurdles, cones, floor sticks/slats and agility jump mats among other items.

Developing Agility and Rotational Speed for Rugby and Football

The drills that follow are but a sample of those that could be implemented in the training programmes of football, rugby and tennis athletes who require these specific speed skills.

Exercise 7.4	**Sprint and Cut (Rugby Agility)**

Sprint and Cut

Hold a ball, jog 10m to a cone, then sprint diagonally 10m to another suitably positioned cone. The angle and direction of 'cut' can be changed to develop a full range of agility, speed and acceleration.

Variations

- An additional cone can be placed 10m in front of the second, and another 5m on from that one. On completing their first agility cut, the player slows to reach the third cone and then cuts to the fourth.
- For even greater specificity, the drill could start with the player lying on the ground without a ball, to simulate the match situation of having to get up quickly and into 'play', as happens after a tackle or a ruck. Additionally, a rugby skill could be performed after the first or second cut, for example, a pass or a kick.

Exercise 7.5   Football Cone Dribble

Football Cone Dribble

Simple, but effective. The player dribbles in and out of cones, placed various distances apart over 15m.

Variations

- Precede the above drill with a sprint to receive a pass, take the ball under control and then dribble through the cones.
- Dribble the ball in a straight line for 20m as fast as possible then adjust over 5m to dribble through cones.
- To simulate a match situation, another player could be tasked with 'chasing' the dribbling player in an attempt to put them off. Note: They should not make a tackle.

Further Useful Sources of Information for the Speed Athlete/coach

SAQ

SAQ stands for 'Speed, Agility and Quickness'. SAQ International is one of the world's leading companies to package and market speed-specific training. SAQ produces numerous books on developing speed, agility and quickness and also runs coaching courses. SAQ has worked with many professional, club and international teams and athletes from various sports.

For more information about SAQ, telephone (01664) 810101 or visit their website at www.saqinternational.com. The following books may also be of interest:

A. Pearson, *SAQ Rugby*, A&C Black, 2001
A. Pearson, *SAQ Soccer*, A&C Black, 2006
A. Pearson and S. Naylor, *SAQ Hockey*, A&C Black, 2003

Frappier System

The Frappier system is another specialist speed-development programme. It differs from SAQ-type systems in that it uses specialist mechanical equipment, such as the 'super treadmill' to develop increased running speed, whereas SAQ tends to use more field-based kit. There are more than 100 Frappier speed centres (and 50 rehabilitation centres allied to orthopaedic departments of hospitals) in the US. Currently there is one site in the UK. A recent development has seen the US Olympic Association adopt the Frappier speed system. It now puts all its young sprinters and 800m, 1500m, 5000m and 10,0000m runners through Frappier programmes. Contact Frappier System UK c/o Sportdimensions, Prebend

Gardens, Chiswick, London, telephone (020) 8563 0007 or visit their website at www.sportdimensions.com.

How Much Do Specialist Agility-developing Programmes and Drills Improve Agility?

Investing in SAQ practices and attending Frappier training sessions can be costly in terms of time and money, so do they actually achieve what they claim? A team of researchers attempted to find out, looking specifically at the use of SAQ techniques and their effect on female football players.

Three groups of matched players were put through different physical conditioning programmes over a 12-week period. Two groups did SAQ training, while the other (active group) carried out their regular sessions. The results:

- All three interventions decreased the participants' body mass index (–3.7 per cent) and fat percentage (–1.7 per cent), and increased flexibility (+14.7 per cent) and VO2max (18.4 per cent).
- However, the SAQ groups showed significantly greater benefits from their training programme than the active group on the sprint to fatigue test and – crucially, in the light of the system's claims – the 25m sprint and left and right side agility tests. (Reference: *J. of Sport Science*, 2004 Feb; 22(2): 191–203)

This research indicates that SAQ and similar specific speed and agility drills and practices must be a constant feature of the training programmes for athletes whose sports require dynamic movements.

Sports Training Tip

Rest is a crucial training variable for the out-and-out speed athlete, as is crafting a training programme that cycles intensities of training to bring about their ultimate ability to express speed. Sprinting flat-out every workout would soon lead to lack of progress and eventual injury. The coach must cycle training, perhaps incorporating a 'slower' week every third week in the main speed development macrocycle (see part 8 for more detail on training planning and an example of a speed training pyramid plan for a sprinter).

Over-speed training

Improving out-and-out speed is no easy task, particularly for the mature athlete. Over-speed training provides a potential way to achieve this. Over-speed training basically allows the athlete to perform a sports skill at a faster pace than normally achievable.

The Rationale for Over-speed Training

Physically, the increase in speed generated by over-speed sprint/agility/throwing training methods is believed to have a lasting effect on muscles' ability to generate force, such as during the foot strike and drive phase of sprinting. Put simply, muscles become more powerful and faster at contracting.

Neurally, over-speed training will 'teach' the brain to fire muscles faster and recruit more muscle (crucially, fast twitch muscle fibres) to achieve greater speeds.

How to Get the Most from Over-speed Training

Outdoor Downhill Over-speed Method

Ideal set-up: Use a dry, non-bumpy grass area that permits the athlete to sprint 20m on the flat (to accelerate to near maximum speed), sprint 15m down a one-degree slope and sprint 15m on the flat (to allow for the continuation of increased speed without the assistance of gravity). Progress gradually; for example, the athlete should run at 75 per cent effort in preliminary workouts and not wear spiked shoes (if applicable) until they have adapted to the demands of the workout.

Towing Methods, including Bungees

Ideal set-up: Use a bungee 20–25m long. This should be secured tightly around the athlete's waist and to an immovable object (such as a football goal post). The athlete walks back to tension the bungee. The further they walk back, the greater the tension that is produced; 25m is a good starting point, allowing runs initially at about 75 per cent of effort to be performed.

Progress is made over a number of workouts until sufficient confidence and condition is developed to allow flat-out and eventually over-speed sprints to be performed. As with down-hill running, the athlete should wear spikes only once suitable confidence and condition is developed, again where appropriate. To develop the over-speed condition, the athlete should back up 30–35m to create the necessary tension in the bungee.

Patented pulley-based towing systems that allow athletes to tow each other or be towed to over-speed performance offer greater safety than bungees, primarily because they afford the athlete the opportunity to 'bail out' safely on a run. However, these can be very expensive.

Over-speed Agility

To achieve multi-directional over-speed agility, the athlete should position themselves backwards or sideways to the direction of pull when using a bungee, then move in the direction of the pull, performing the requisite sport's skill, such as side steps.

Treadmill Methods

Ideal condition: The decline of the treadmill should be 2 per cent.

The potential advantages of treadmill running include:

- Speed can be systematically and progressively controlled throughout a workout and across the developmental training programme.
- The coach can stand alongside the athlete while they are in full flow and provide immediate verbal feedback.
- Some speed treadmills (such as the Frappier super treadmill) enable the coach to physically correct the athlete from the side, for example, by using a carefully placed hand to the small of the athlete's back while they are in motion to help keep the athlete's hips 'high' (a key aspect of sprint technique) and assist them with keeping up with the required belt speed.

The ideal conditions for downhill outdoor and towing methods are adapted from G. Dintimen and B. Ward, *Sports Speed*, Human Kinetics, 2003.

Sports Training Tips: Over-speed Training

Perform Unassisted Efforts in the Same Session

Unassisted runs/sport skills should always be performed in the same training session as over-speed works. This will help the athlete learn how to fire their muscles at increased speeds, rather than simply being 'dragged' to achieving remarkable sprint/agility performances. Research indicates that athletes will run faster unassisted immediately after over-speed runs. However, this window of opportunity may exist for only 10 minutes or so, which means you should not delay! This could be worth experimenting with before competitions. See page 105 for details on Potentiation

Keep Over-speed Speed to within 10 per cent of Unassisted Speed

This should provide the best conditions to ensure the athlete's neuromuscular system is optimally stimulated by their own efforts. Achieving greater than 10 per cent over-speed speeds is non-productive because the athlete will not be fully in control of what they are doing. Additionally, they may be forced to adopt an incorrect sprinting posture in an attempt to stop themselves falling.

Throwing Lighter Balls to Develop a More Powerful Throwing Arm

Increasing arm speed can be a key determinant of performance in sports such as cricket, baseball and the athletic throwing events. One of the most effective ways of doing this is through the use of lighter (and heavier) implements and balls. However, as with over-speed running, throwing greater distances and achieving greater arm speeds with lighter implements will be of little benefit if the 'new speed' is not channelled into actual 'real time' performance. To ensure this does not happen, athlete and coach should not perform prolonged periods of throwing lighter balls/implements within a training period without experiencing the real thing. Research has shown that the following type of workout is particularly useful in improving throwing arm speed.

On a set by set basis:
1. Throw implement 5 per cent heavier than standard implement.
2. Throw implement 5–10 per cent lighter than normal weight.
3. Throw normal-weight implement.

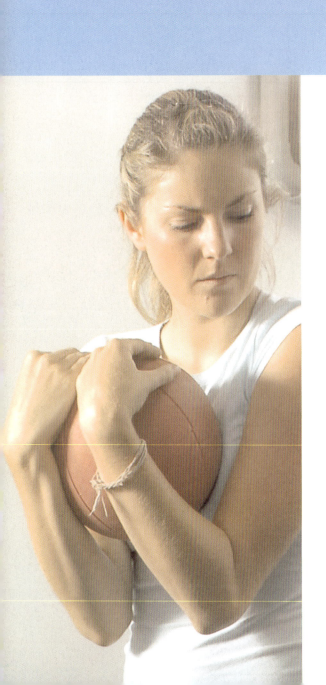

PART **EIGHT**

TRAINING PLANNING

To maximise sports performance, athlete/athletes (as in a team) need to train systematically, placing the varying sports-conditioning training ingredients (weight-training, plyometrics, power combination training and so on) into an ordered methodology – a training plan. Failure to develop such a plan, complete with appropriate goals and monitoring, will prevent optimum performance being achieved. This could also lead to staleness (due to a lack of rest), and increase the risk of injury. In this part I provide a simple model of how to plan for sport, 'the training pyramid', while outlining more advanced 'periodisation' techniques and opinions.

Without knowing where the athlete is going and what they will have to do along the way to get there, there is every possibility that the athlete will fail to get anywhere near their desired sporting goals.

Sports Training Tip

Coach/athlete should never lose sight of the importance of evaluating training. This process will enable the most effective returns from training to be achieved. Training progress and the 'health' of the athlete can be continually monitored and adjustments made to the training plan as necessary.

Goal-setting and Training Planning

Establishing a sports goal, or set of goals, is central to determining the delivery of the training plan. Examples of training goals for different sports include:

- **Sprinter.** Reducing 100m time by 0.2 seconds and running the improved time by August (or whenever the main competition/peak is required).
- **Football goalkeeper.** Improving shot reaction and jumping power during pre-season and maintaining it throughout the season.
- **Racket sports player.** Improving turning ability before the grass court season and maintaining and adapting it for the subsequent hard court season.
- **Distance runner.** Improving end-of-race sprint for a series of key races throughout the autumn.

SMARTER Goal-setting

A very simple way of establishing a sports goal is to use the SMARTER set of princi-ples. The athlete's goal should be established against the following principles, which will ensure they are optimally shaped. Goals should be:

S   specific
M   measurable
A   agreed
R   realistic
T   targeted
E   empowering
R   revisable

Considering these goal-setting principles in more detail:

- **Specific.** A goal must be focused and targeted. An athlete saying 'I want to run faster' is of little use as this is likely either to limit improvement or overestimate potential.
- **Measurable.** It is crucial for sports goals to be measurable. The 100m goal I gave earlier, for example, has an obvious competitive target. Objective training/competition goals must be established, and measured by specifically designed workouts and tests to progress the athlete towards their main goal. Consequently, there should also be main and sub-goals that are progressed through on the way to the main competitive goal; again, these need to be objectively measurable.
- **Achievable.** There is no point setting an unattainable goal. Athlete/coach must consider training maturity, lifestyle, training options and facilities and so on, in order to establish appropriate (and achievable) goals.
- **Realistic.** Sports goals must fit the athlete's lifestyle and those whose lives are affected by the athlete, for example, partners and work colleagues. Training has to complement everyday life, not work against it. (It may be easier for full- or part-time athletes to achieve such a balance than those who work full-time and have family commitments; however,

being a full-time athlete can have its own problems.)

- **Targeted.** It seems obvious that sports goals must be targeted, but many coaches and athletes do not actually line up their training efforts. Instead, they operate without a distinct direction, which has a knock-on effect on virtually all other aspects of their sports training. The best way to avoid this and ensure that goals are targeted is to:

- construct a relevant and progressive training plan with a designated time frame (including goals!);
- constantly ask the question, 'will this training really benefit my sports training goals?' during every stage of the preparation and competition process – after all, there is no point in wasting training effort (or doing too much, which impairs rather than improves performance).

- **Empowering.** Pursuing and achieving sports goals must be a positive process. The athlete (and the coach) must value what they are striving for. If they do not then disillusionment can creep in and motivation wane.
- **Revisable.** This is perhaps the most important SMARTER principle when applied to sports training. The goals of the athlete/coach must not be set in stone. They need to be adaptable in response to both positive and negative circumstances. If, for example, the athlete becomes ill or sustains an injury, or progresses more quickly than expected, goals will have to be revised.

Sports Training Tip

Athlete/coach should establish short-, medium- and long-term goals to optimally shape the sports training process. These should meet all aspects of training and competitive requirements.

Being a Full-time Athlete

I indicated that being a full-time athlete can allow for greater physical and mental focus when considering the SMARTER goal-setting principles. Although this is true for many, having too much time to train can be problematic because the athlete can develop a one-track focus and perhaps not keep their lives in perspective. Consequently, many coaches recommend that full-time athletes do something else as well, perhaps a part-time course of study or even a part-time job. Positive distractions are needed.

Injury and Potential Solutions for Full-time (and Part-time) Athletes

Here is an example of why too much focus on sports training can be detrimental. Very recently, there has been a re-evaluation of, in particular, the neural consequences of injury. Research has begun to indicate that many athletes still suffer pain when their injury's physical symptoms have cleared up. This is referred to as 'maladaptive' pain. It is as if they are still 'thinking' that they are injured when they are not.

When a full-time athlete sustains an injury, it can literally collapse their world – as their world may only be sport. They may dwell on the injury and often worry constantly about how it is responding and when it will be okay to start training again. On the other hand, an athlete who has 'other' life demands will have less time to worry and may have less opportunity to create a 'pain blueprint'.

It is important that the athlete (whether full-time or part-time) adopts a positive approach to injury – if and when sustained – and literally learns how to train the brain to beat injury.

Selected Symptoms of Maladaptive Pain

• Although the injury has healed physically, pain persists, often far greater than the injury warrants.
• Athlete needs to go through a detailed physical rehabilitation process in order to 'convince' themselves that the 'injury is getting better'.

Adaptive pain produces athlete behaviour that promotes recovery. The athlete believes, for example, that the pain is there to warn them not to train, that it is subsiding and that it will eventually go completely. Athlete/coach and relevant medical practitioners should be aware of the need to encourage this positive mental state in the athlete. Negativity will breed the potential for maladaptive pain to worsen. (Further mental approaches for maximising sports potential are provided in part 9.)

Testing

Testing and evaluation play a key role in training planning and successful sports conditioning. There are a myriad of tests available to athletes and their coaches. Some are standard, such as VO2max and heart rate maximum, and establishing weight-training one repetition maximums and plyometric best tests. It is beyond the scope of this book to outline all the tests that the athlete/coach could use. But, as befits the overall theme of successful sports training, those the coach/athlete decide to use should be specific – to the athlete, the time of the training/competitive period and, of course, the athlete's sport.

Athlete Profile: Cathy Freeman, Olympic 400m Champion – on Testing

Freeman had a number of specific sessions that she used regularly to test how her preparation was going. One of these required her to run 6 × 200m on the track with recoveries that decreased from five minutes to one minute between runs. Freeman explained that when she approached peak performance, she would be able to complete all runs in under 25 seconds.

As coach/athlete, you should select a session that is particularly relevant to the needs of your sport and time in the training year and repeat it at regular intervals – perhaps every four to six weeks – to gauge how training is progressing.

Training Planning Models

The Soviet sports scientist, Matveyev, pioneered modern periodisation theory in the 1960s. Periodisation basically refers to a phased, systematic, quantitative and scientific approach to training. His work has subsequently been reinterpreted and modified to produce different periodisation models for various sports. All models aim to achieve the optimum conditions for peak sports performance. Under the 'classic' Matveyev model, the training year is divided into distinct phases – you will have noted references to these on occasions throughout this text. Dependent on their duration, these phases are termed 'macro-', 'meso-' and 'microcyles'. Each progresses the athlete through to a peak or peaks. As a rough guide, macrocycles last months, mesocycles weeks, and microcycles days.

Within each cycle, the key training variables of volume, intensity and specificity and so on (see page 163) are manipulated to achieve a designated training effect.

The training pyramid that follows is a simple way for coach/athlete to understand basic periodisation.

The Training Pyramid

One of the easiest ways to shape a sports training plan is to view it as a 'pyramid'. The base provides the foundation upon which more specific levels of training are built. These progress the athlete through to the apex, where peak sports performance will be produced in training and competition.

The training pyramid method of training planning tends to work best for sports with a definite peak, such as track and field. Each phase should last at least six weeks and at most 16 weeks (as sports scientists have noted that these durations are long enough to promote positive and lasting physiological adaptation).

Getting into top shape for a sport with more than one peak, particularly one with multiple playing requirements like football, is a more difficult proposition and requires modified training planning (see 'Undulating Periodisation', page 166).

Sample Training Pyramid

What follows is an example of a basic training pyramid for a sprint athlete, with a single peak. Coach/athlete should study it to develop an understanding of how to put training phases (the pyramid levels) together to optimise, in this case, speed. Each phase should be designed to 'lift' the athlete's speed and fitness from level to level, safely and effectively. I have provided an overview/indication of the type of training that the sprinter could be performing during each phase, as well as suggested phase durations. Note that the training sessions in each phase will themselves evolve as the phases progress and the sprinter's specific fitness and preparation increases.

The sprint athlete's sample speed pyramid

has three distinct training phases and one rest and recovery phase. However, athlete/coach could design a pyramid with more training phases, if their training and competitive goals are specific enough to warrant it.

Sample Training Pyramid for Sprint Athlete
Most of the workout suggestions given here have been described elsewhere in the book.

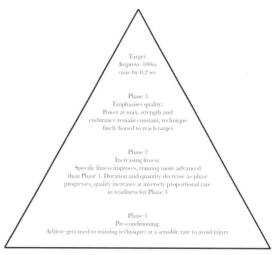

Target:
Improve 100m
time by 0.2 sec

Phase 3
Emphasises quality:
Power at max, strength and
endurance remain constant, technique
finely honed to reach target

Phase 2
Increasing fitness:
Specific fitness improves, training more advanced
than Phase 1. Duration and quantity decrease as phase
progresses, quality increases at inversely proportional rate
in readiness for Phase 3

Phase 1
Pre-conditioning:
Athlete gets used to training techniques at a sensible rate to avoid injury

Phase 4: Low-key training and relaxation, recovery from previous season in readiness for Phase 1

Phase 1
Key characteristics. This phase is designed to build a suitable, in this case, speed base. It normally emphasises the progressive development of training quantity, where the athlete 'trains to train' and pre-conditions to build against potential injury. Quality increases as the phase progresses. For those new to (speed) training, this phase is about getting used to training, initially slowly and safely, while developing sound technique.

Suggested workout options:

- 300/200/100m at 60–70% effort x 2 with 3 min recovery between runs and 5 min between sets
- 150m split into 50m accelerate, 50m relax, 50m fast x 4, with 4 min recovery between runs
- Sprint starts introduced towards the end of the phase, but emphasising technique rather than speed
- Bounding and hopping over 20–30m, with reps increasing as the phase progresses but with full recovery
- Power combination training with an endurance emphasis, e.g. 6 complexes – 12 weight reps at 60% 1RM and 12 associated plyometric repetitions, 4–6 sets, incomplete recovery
- Pre-conditioning workouts (*see* part 2)
- Circuit resistance training
- Drills performed as part of other workouts and as sessions in their own right. The emphasis should be on the mastery of technique, with speed of movement being less important.

Duration: 6–16 weeks

As I indicated previously, the work done in these training phases would be progressive and cyclical. Rest (*see* page 163) would also be carefully programmed in to avoid over-training and injury.

Phase 2
Key characteristics. The athlete becomes increasingly and specifically fitter in this phase than in the previous one and can handle much more advanced training options and workouts. Duration and quantity are greatest at the beginning of this phase, but normally decline as phase three approaches. Conversely, quality increases as the phase progresses.

Suggested workout options:

- Weights – increase the amount lifted while reducing the number of reps. Introduce more sport-specific and advanced training methods, such as step-up drives and power combination training respectively. The latter should use heavier loadings than in phase 1 but with fewer reps, e.g. 6 complexes with weights at 80% 1RM, 4–6 repetitions and 4 x 6 plyometrics.
- Circuit resistance training sessions – number of circuits/reps reduced as the training phase progresses to allow for greater quality
- 90/100/120/130/140/150m runs at 80% effort with 4-6 min recovery between runs
- 90m, split into 30 accelerate, 30 relax, 30 fast x 6; 4 min recovery between runs
- Sprint starts, with emphasis on technical execution, building up intensity as the phase progresses, plus other acceleration training
- Uphill sprints, e.g. 2 x 4 x 40m from standing, walk back recovery with 5 min between sets
- Plyometric workouts with the emphasis on speed of movement and forward travel. This phase, for example, could see the transition in emphasis from bounds to speed bounds.
- Drills performed as part of session or as a complete workout in their own right. In terms of progression, these should introduce speedier movements.
- Pre-conditioning exercises maintained as part of other workouts and warm-up

Duration: 12–16 weeks

Phase 3
Key characteristics. This phase usually emphasises quality as the athlete reaches their speed goal. They will be able to complete workouts at a much faster pace than when they first started speed training. Power will

max out and they will maintain rather than improve strength and endurance. Competitions will be introduced, and should be carefully selected to bring the sprinter to a peak. Too many can leave the athlete tired, while too few can leave them 'ring rusty'. Sprinters, unlike, for example, marathon runners, can compete relatively frequently. However, a point will still be reached when mental and physical fatigue negatively affects their performance.

Suggested workout options:

- Rolling 40m sprints with full recovery
- One power combination training workout a week: 4 exercises, 6 reps x 2 sets (weight exercises at 75% 1RM)
- Sprint starts: 6 x 20m with full recovery
- Three 120m runs at 80% effort with emphasis on relaxed technique, full recovery
- Sprint drills session utilising agility and fast feet drills
- Over-speed session, e.g. 4 x 60m downhill sprints with full recovery
- Pre-conditioning exercises maintained as part of other workouts and warm-ups

Duration: 6–8 weeks

Phase 4
Key characteristics. This is a recovery or relaxed training phase, used before returning to phase 1 at the end of the training year/competition period. It is designed to allow body and mind time to regenerate.

During this phase the athlete could participate in different sports and recreational fitness activities, but on a very low-key basis. Speed (and most sport training) activities are very taxing and can stress the body, and it is crucial to allow ample time for recuperation during this phase. Holidays could, for example, be taken during this period.

Duration: 4–8 weeks

Sports Training Tip

Continuous evaluation is a crucial part of successful training planning. However, the tests used by coach/athlete must be relevant. The athlete must be rested before performing them, if they are to be meaningful. Tests should be scheduled in at appropriate points in a training pyramid (periodisation plan); the beginning, middle and end of each training phase are good times to assess progression in this respect. Competitions can also be used as a means to assess performance and ready the athlete on the way to their peak.

Creating a sports training plan is like following a recipe. All the coach/athlete needs to do is select from the right sports performance-enhancing ingredients, prepare and blend these together in the best possible way (via a training plan) to achieve optimum results.

Adaptation and Rest

As indicated, adaptation describes the positive changes that occur in an athlete's body when it is consistently subjected to regular training. Rest is as crucial to this process as the actual training itself, because it is during the periods when the athlete is *not* training that positive physiological changes are made. Note: This does not mean that training should cease on 'rest' days – although I recommend at least one day of complete recovery a week for athletes, regardless of sport – rather that training intensities should be manipulated. Easy, medium and hard workouts should be cycled to keep the athlete fresh, healthy and progressing.

Recovery Strategies

Sports Massage

A regular massage from a sports therapist or masseur will aid soft tissue recovery. It is more than possible that muscles will have developed sore spots, created by previous injuries. This 'scar' tissue can make muscles prone to further injury. It is important that this tissue is prevented from causing unnecessary problems. Regular sports massage will literally rub these out, realign muscle fibres and aid the removal of toxins.

Warming Down after Training

Bringing the body back down to a more steady state after a workout will promote recovery and reduce subsequent injury. Most warm-downs utilise a period of easy cardiovascular activity and gentle stretches.

Heat and Ice Treatments

Immediate recovery treatments, like ice baths, are a regular feature of professional sports set-ups. They offer speedier recovery and injury reduction. All athletes and their coaches, whatever their level, should adopt a similar proactive approach. If you do not have the necessary facilities on hand, try the following.

When showering, alternate hot and cold water on your upper and lower legs (or other exercised parts). Spray cold water for two minutes and hot for one minute. This alternate heat therapy will increase blood flow through muscles and assist the removal of waste products.

A Good Night's Sleep

Regular sleep greatly assists sports training adaptation. It is difficult to be precise about the amount of sleep needed, but at least eight hours should be aimed for. Numerous regenerative processes occur while sleeping, particularly in the deepest periods, such as growth hormone release.

All athletes should make their bedtime routines consistent and their bedroom a relaxing environment. They should literally switch off when they switch off the lights, so that they can switch on when they perform their sports training.

The Training Variables

The so-called training variables of volume, intensity, duration, rest and frequency determine the balance of training, as indicated in relation to the sport training pyramid model (*see* page 159). If the training pyramid provides the basic recipe for developing/optimising speed then the variables provide the cooking times and temperatures for bringing the menu (training plan) to life.

Volume

Volume simply means the *amount* of work carried out in a particular training period or session. It can be measured in terms of time, numbers of repetitions or ground contacts (the latter for plyometric workouts) or the amount of weight lifted. Volume is strongly influenced by intensity and duration. Note that in the sprint training pyramid example provided, phase 1 places the greatest emphasis on volume. This base-building phase of training is the time when the sprinter completes more distance on the track and lifts more weight. In comparison, for an endurance athlete following a base-building training programme, mileage might actually increase right up to the competitive phase of the training plan.

Intensity

Intensity refers to the level of effort required for a workout, or part of a workout. For example, a flat-out sprint would be deemed to be performed at 100 per cent intensity. A circuit resistance or interval training workout could also be performed at 100 per cent intensity, although the training effect would be very different – it would generate greater fatigue because of the different energy pathway being trained.

To ensure the steady progression of adaptation to training, performance percentages can be established to determine the intensity of workouts, as illustrated in the training pyramid. On the track, for example, these can be worked out in relation to a runner's best times. As indicated in part 4, percentages for 1RM can be similarly established for weight-training workouts.

Duration

Duration is the length of a component of a workout or a training phase. Intensity and duration work together to create vastly different types of workout, as shown in the following example.

A rower could either:

- row for 30 minutes at low intensity (22 strokes per minute at 80 per cent HRMax) to maintain aerobic fitness or
- perform 10 x 1 minute intervals at 90 per cent effort* (32 plus SPM at 90 per cent plus HRMax), with 90 seconds' recovery between each interval to improve lactate tolerance and endurance speed.

Thus, two completely different sessions can be created simply by manipulating the intensity and duration variables.

You will see from the speed training pyramid that the work of the sprinter becomes more intense (faster in this case), and the duration of efforts (runs) generally shorter as the apex of the pyramid approaches. This is because the athlete needs to be running as fast as possible at the start of and throughout the main competitive season.

Rest

Rest takes place between workouts or between elements of a single workout, such as the plyometric and weight-training components of a power combination session. Whatever the situation, rest must be carefully controlled. As indicated, this training variable is crucial if optimum physiological adaptation to training is to occur. Too little and too much rest will impair immediate and long-term training response.

Athlete/coach should not be fooled into thinking that 'the longer the rest the less intense the workout will be'. Performing 6 x 60m sprints at 100 per cent intensity, with a full recovery, makes for a very tough workout because of the strain placed on body and mind, despite the length of recovery.

Frequency

Frequency refers to the number of times an athlete trains over a designated training period, or the number of times a specific type of training, such as weights, is used.

Although it may not be readily apparent from the training pyramid, the frequency of training sessions would normally reduce as important competitions approach. This enables the athlete to peak.

Coach/athlete may also reduce the frequency

---

* The rower's 90 per cent intensity would be calculated from their best 90-second flat-out rowing time.

of specific training sessions, such as weight-training ones, and increase the frequency of others, such as over-speed ones, to bring about more specific adaptation towards a peak, in this case for a sprint athlete.

Sports Training Tip

The timing of training workouts and their proximity to one another and competition is crucial when maximising performance. The human body cannot improve continuously. For example, training for out-and-out speed every day for six weeks would soon bring an athlete to a performance plateau – assuming they did not burn themselves out mentally or sustain an injury in the process. Training needs to be cycled carefully, and intensity adjusted accordingly, for optimum training gains to ensue.

Endurance athletes are prone to ignoring the need for recovery. They will often go for a run before a race, or think that more training (on top of an already high mileage!) will increase their performance. This is not necessarily the case or good for performance.

All athletes would be wise to heed this advice, especially if their training up to an important competition has gone well: 'one more training session is unlikely to make a big difference'. It is better to get to a competition fresh and uninjured.

Sports Training Tip

A training plan should be both flexible and adaptable (see the SMARTER goal planner, revisable aspect). Plans may need to be revised in the light of injury, for example. At such time, the coach needs to call on all their practical and motivational skills to keep their athlete as performance-ready as possible, without risk of further injury. In consequence, they may need to seek advice from relevant professionals, such as physiotherapists (see *also* 'Maladaptive Pain', page 157).

Catabolic and Anabolic Effects of Training

Physiologically, one of the prime effects of sports training is the breakdown of muscle protein. In the process of weight-training, power athletes break down muscle protein. This regenerates during recovery in conjunction with optimum diet, thus increasing muscular strength and size. This is an example of the 'anabolic effect' of training. However, too much training and insufficient recovery – particularly for endurance athletes – can lead to muscle protein being broken down and not replenished (largely as a consequence of protein being used as energy). This results in muscle shrinkage (atrophy), and potential loss of power, known as the 'catabolic effect'. Coaches and athletes from all sports must be mindful to maintain training conditions that optimise protein growth and re-synthesis. (Suitable dietary suggestions are found in part 10.)

Competition and Peaking

Competitions, by their very nature, stress the body to a much greater extent than training. It is usual for an athlete to feel 'drained' after a competition. This will be to a far greater extent than after a 100-per-cent intensity training session, for example. The main cause is increased stress and mental demand. It is therefore crucial for coach and athlete to devise an optimum competition schedule. This should include a mixture of low-key events and major competitions. It often helps if there is a sense of 'build-up', mentally as well as physically, towards the main competition.

Note: Young athletes or less mature adults (in terms of training experience) can benefit from greater competition frequency. For such athletes, competitions serve to improve performance and condition until they have developed both base fitness and competitive experience. Further thoughts on the mental aspects of competition are provided in part 9.

Periodisation

I noted that periodisation is the term used in the sports science world for the optimum and systematic preparation of an athlete for sport over a training period. Again as noted, the training pyramid is a form of periodisation. The pyramid is specifically an example of what sports scientists call a 'single periodisation' training plan. This is when the athlete progresses towards a single peak, or at least a single competitive period in which peak condition is sought.

Double Periodisation

Some sports, such as track and field, have more than one competitive season – for example, an indoor season and an outdoor one. This allows the athlete to train for at least two peaks. In such circumstances, an athlete is said to be following a 'double periodisation' plan.

In its simplest form, double periodisation is like adding two training pyramids together. The athlete works through one pyramid, competes (although not in all cases), peaks (or comes close to a physiological peak), rests (or performs at a much reduced level of training) and then begins another training pyramid. The time frames for each pyramid are worked back from important competitions and adjusted accordingly. However, things are a little more complicated in reality, as a sprinter, for example, will not start the second training pyramid at the same levels of strength, speed and power as they did the first. Thus, with double periodisation, the training variables are manipulated to bring about optimum performance in an overlapping and undulating fashion. Table 8.1 shows how this is achieved.

Double Periodisation Can Bring Greater Performance Gains

Double periodisation has been shown to enhance speed and power in sports with clearly defined seasons because of the way the training elements combine to specifically condition and lift the body's performance capability. Research from the former Soviet Union showed that, with double periodisation, a mature (in training years) sprinter could expect a 1.55 per cent improvement over the year, compared with just 0.96 per cent with a single periodisation programme. For high jumpers, the estimated difference was even more startling: 2.4 per cent for single periodisation, more than doubling to 5.05 per cent for double periodisation.

However, it was also recommended that a single periodisation programme be followed every four years or so to allow for base fitness to be topped up and improved.

Table 8.1	Double versus Single Periodised Training Schematic											
Double		1				2		2				
Single												
Month	Nov	Dec	Jan	Feb	Mar	Apr	May	June	July	Aug	Sep	Oct

Key
Dark red/red = preparation macrocycle 1
Orange/mid-orange = specific preparation
Yellow/mid- and light yellow = competition-specific macrocycle
Blue = rest/recovery macrocycle

Note: The exact training balance would not remain the same in each macrocycle. I have used the dark to light colouring to illustrate graphically that the training should evolve, bringing in more specific work.

Double Periodisation Model
This example of a double periodisation model would suit a sprinter who is aiming to achieve near peak 60m form in March for the indoor season and then a second maximum competitive peak in August/September for 100m championship running. As indicated, double periodisation may have advantages over single periodisation for achieving enhanced performance for speed and power sports with clearly defined competitive seasons.

Single Periodisation Model
This example of a single periodisation plan could apply to a sprint or field event athlete who is aiming to achieve peak performance for a major championship in August/September. Despite the advantages of double periodisation

for certain sports, following a single periodisation plan every fourth year or so is recommended to aid recovery and build greater base condition.

General Comment
Each phase of preparation in both periodisation models would largely reflect the percentage of general, specific and competition-specific training performed by the athlete. Each would build upon its predecessor.

Each macrocycle would contain specific mesocycles and microcycles designed to further the preparation and peaking of the athlete. These would be planned in great detail as they approached.

Team Sport Training Planning and Undulating Periodisation

One of the main criticisms of periodisation is that it is seen to work well only with sports that have clearly defined seasons, such as track and field, and again with sports such as track and field that have highly quantifiable training elements. I now describe ways and methods that allow periodisation to be applied to other sports with longer playing seasons, multiple competitions and more qualitative demands.

Training Players in Field Sports Differently

Coaches should realise the necessity of training players differently according to position if they want to maximise team performance, even though it can be logistically difficult. I have provided some research from the world of rugby union to exemplify why this is so.

A focus was made on 29 elite players over eight matches in the New Zealand 'Super 12 season'. The researchers discovered (among various findings) that front row and back row forwards completed more high-intensity efforts than backs, with the former getting on average only 35 seconds' recovery between efforts. From a training perspective this means that these players should perform more high-intensity intervals than backs in training, with shorter periods of low-intensity activity in between. The forwards' training would emphasise the development of the short-term anaerobic energy system over the immediate anaerobic system. Backs, on the other hand, especially wingers, would benefit more from a greater emphasis on training the immediate energy pathway. (Reference: *Peak Performance*, 2003 Aug.; 185: pp. 4–6)

Those involved in team sports face a myriad of issues that complicate periodisation. This is due to the length and intensity of the playing season and often, in the case of the professional sports, the need to field the best players most of the time. The 2001 British Lions rugby tour to Australia, managed by Graham Henry, is a case in point. The players arrived 'down under' after a tough domestic and international season. They also had a very tough tour itinerary, yet for reasons best known to the coaching staff, they were subjected to a highly demanding training programme. It was as if, within a very short space of time, a mini periodisation mesocycle was being implemented, perhaps with too much general and specific training. Two, even three workouts a day were regular occurrences, many of which were full-contact. The latter resulted in a number of injuries to key players, such as Dan Luger and Mike Catt.

The following section examines the best times to develop condition for athletes involved in long multiple-competition sports.

The Best Time to Develop Condition for Team Sports Players

For team sports, pre-season or in-season breaks may be the best, indeed only, time to improve physical condition. Trying to do this during in-season training or at the end of a highly demanding season can be detrimental. At these times, maintenance of condition, rather than enhancement of it, is the key.

Researchers studied 14 professional and 15 college-aged rugby league players over 29 weeks in-season in an attempt to determine whether maximum strength and power could be increased concurrently while attempting to balance the demands of playing and recovery. All players performed training aimed at increasing strength, power, speed and endurance.

It was discovered that the players' performances remained unchanged over the season for the majority of the tests. This led the authors to believe that the prioritisation, sequencing and timing of the training sessions kept the players in prime rugby league playing condition. This they attributed to the use of undulating periodisation (UP). (Reference: *J. of Strength Cond. Res.*, 2001 May, 15(2) 198–209)

The implication of this research for coaches is that they should develop a strong foundation of condition pre-season and then use UP methods to maintain it throughout.

Squad Rotation

Squad rotation offers another means of maximising team performance. However, coach and athlete must be in harmony if this approach is to be used – chairmen, fans, player injuries and the overall success of the team can always throw a spanner in the works.

What is Undulating Periodisation?

Undulating periodisation (UP) combines much shorter training phases (days/weeks) with different modes of exercise and exercise intensity. Basically, the various ingredients in the training mix are cooked up at the same time. One workout could emphasise speed and power, the next skill and the following endurance, and so on. Although it may seem random, it is not; the coach will have to be highly competent to maintain optimum condition using UP. They will probably, for example, have baseline fitness requirements for individual players, and will attempt to maintain these across the season.

Skill/strength Periodisation

As noted in part 4, developing greater strength in the weights room does not guarantee improved performance. One of the reasons could be that skill becomes divorced from strength, power and speed. A tennis player, for example, may develop more shoulder, trunk and leg power, yet be unable to serve any quicker. In all likelihood, the reason will be a lack of attention to skill development – the tennis serve – during the periodisation process. Consequently, the player (and all other athletes) should never lose touch with the serving action (or their specific sporting skills). If relevant practices are included in the training plan, there will be much less likelihood of power and strength gains outstripping skill.

Skill/strength periodisation is so designed to continually marry the development of strength (or any other physical component) to skill. In its purest form, the model develops skill in a macrocycle at the beginning of the training year (and then constantly throughout the training period), so that it is cemented into the athlete before and as more power, and so on, is added. Doing this should allow the athlete to apply their developing physical components optimally.

Periodisation – Further Thoughts for Those in More Qualitative Sports

Some sports, like the martial arts, although supremely technical, are seemingly more qualitative in their development of physical condition. Although judo players will, for example, strength train, they obviously need to fight and perform judo-specific skills as the mainstay of their training.

For judo, the Polish sports scientist Sikorski devised 11 general and 23 judo-specific drills for the national team based on lactate and heart rate response. This enabled coaches to plan a Matveyev periodisation-style programme for their judo players – players' condition and their training are made quantifiable and can be so progressed.

Others in judo regard time on the mat (time doing judo) as the key element of the training variable volume. As the competition macrocycle approaches, more time is spent practising the sport and less on general conditioning. Although this may seem obvious, it is surprising how many coaches (whatever their sport) neglect this prime need and become preoccupied with developing strength, endurance and power at the expense of skill. As indicated, skill must never be neglected, whatever the sport.

Conditioning Drills for Different Team-playing Positions

Conditioning drills can also be constructed that closely replicate the playing requirements of different team-playing positions. Here, I use rugby as an example again.

Rugby union forwards: 6 x power cleans at 80 per cent 1RM; 10 press-ups from unstable base (one hand on medicine ball); 10m sprint.

30 seconds' recovery between each set – repeat 10 times.

Rugby union backs: 10 press-ups from unstable base (one hand on medicine ball), pick up ball 15m sprint, slow to stop, put ball down and repeat.

45 seconds' recovery between each set – repeat 8 times.

(See also part 7.)

Sports Training Tip

Coaches of players in contact sports should be mindful of performing too much contact work, especially in-season. This will in all likelihood increase the risk of injury. Practices must be developed that replicate playing conditions as much as possible, but minimise injury risk. Flag and touch rugby comes to mind for those in these sports. Wearing suitable padding and using floor mats and softer tackle bags are additional means for rugby players and those involved in combat sports. Throwing powerbags or medicine balls and catching them, either individually or between athletes, is a further means to develop the athlete's ability to 'take' contact, while minimising injury risk.

Mental Periodisation

Just as the body is physically progressed through periodised training programmes, so too must the mind be prepared. In doing so the athlete should reflect on what their goals are at a particular time in the training year, even the goal of a specific session. Such focus will bring about optimum conditions for the continued achievement of peak performance when it matters. Part 9 focuses on mental training.

PART **NINE**

TRAINING THE MIND

Mental factors are as influential as physical factors when it comes to winning and losing and achieving peak sporting condition, but despite this they are often overlooked by athlete and coach. In this part I provide numerous key practical mental strategies and techniques that will significantly enhance sports performance.

How to Apply Mental Training

In the following section I provide a practical step-by-step guide for athlete/coach to use to begin the process of applying mental strategies to their training.

Step 1: Identify the Problems That Have Been Hampering Performance

Athlete/coach should begin by identifying the problems that have been hampering performance success and the areas that need to be improved. Performance profiling (PP) is a tool used within sports psychology that can do just this. PP can be applied to all aspects of training, not just the mental ones. It places the athlete centre stage, evaluating themselves rather than being *acted* on by a sports psychologist or coach – although these people can play a useful role in the PP process by assisting its delivery and prompting the athlete. Here's what to do (*see also* Table 9.1).

Athlete/coach should identify the key attributes of a successful performer in their sport. In the example below, I refer to a sprinter. The athlete should spend 5 to 10 minutes reflecting on this and writing down their answers. They may decide that the following (mental) attributes are crucial:

- Appropriate channelling of aggression
- Ability to avoid distraction
- Confidence
- Relaxation
- Dealing with pressure
- Enjoyment

When the athlete has decided on the relevant qualities, they should give each a mark out of 10. This creates what is known as an 'ideal profile' (IP). They may decide that their successful performer scores 10 on most of their IPs.

Next, the athlete should take the IP scores and rate themselves against each, to produce what is called their 'subject self-assessment' (SSA). This is done in relation to an 'ideal self-assessment' state of 10 (ISA). Thus they may believe that they score four in terms of their 'appropriate channelling of aggression'. Basically, they are identifying and acknowledging how they react under competition conditions. They might believe that they become too tense, for example, with knock-on consequences for relaxation when they are sprinting.

A few calculations are then required to determine the athlete's 'discrepancy' (D) score, or more straightforwardly, the areas they need to work on.

Calculations:
- Subtract the SSA from the ISA.
- Multiply this figure by the IP.

Table 9.1	Example of an International Sprinter Constructing a Performance Profile				
Quality (as indentified in elite sprinters)	Ideal profile (IP)	Ideal self-assessment (ISA)	Athlete self-assessment (SSA)	ISA Minus SSA	Discrepancy score (D) (ISA-SSA) x IP
Appropriate channelling of aggression	10	10	4	6	60
Ability to avoid distraction	10	10	8	2	20
Confidence	10	10	8	2	20
Relaxation	10	10	8	2	20
Dealing with pressure	10	10	9	1	10
Enjoyment	10	10	3	7	70

From the table, athlete/coach will be able to see that the example sprinter's PP identifies high discrepancy scores for 'enjoyment' (70) and 'appropriate channelling of aggression' (60). These are therefore the qualities they would need to focus on initially.

Note: Performance profiling can also be used to identify physical areas that need to be improved. Coach/athlete should use PP regularly in order to assess the mental and physical progression of the athlete.

Step 2: Apply the Following Selected Sports Psychology Strategies

There are numerous sports psychology strategies that athlete/coach can use to improve PP and sports performance. For them to be successful they must be worked on with the same diligence as physical training – repetition will bring about success.

1: The Success Cycle (SC) and Goal-setting (GS)

If an athlete has a main goal of medalling in their sport's national championships then they should begin boosting their SC well before they enter the competitive arena.

Works on: Athlete's feelings about themselves and improving competitive performance (improving their self-efficacy, *see* page 180).

How: The athlete decides on their main objectives (use the PP method) then records the workout goal/goals that will enable them to improve. Here's an example for 'appropriate channelling of aggression' for a long jumper:

'I will not be distracted by the crowd. I will benefit from the positive effect that it will have on my performance by increasing my adrenaline and motivation. I will respond in a controlled way.'

The athlete should then write down a key word/words that reflect this goal, perhaps on the back of their hand when training or competing (they can also establish a competition plan). The athlete should then look at this word/words from time to time prior to and during their training workouts or competitions in order to focus and remind themselves of their goals and how they are going to achieve them and get the best out of themselves.

After their workout/competition, athlete/coach should objectively evaluate how the former met their goal/goals by using a scale from 1 to 10. They should record their score (*see* 'Attribution' as a critical way to analyse goal attainment, and page 156 for a detailed consideration of goal-setting).

Note: As with PP, the athlete does not have to select only mental goals to boost their SC. However, the keys from the psychological perspective are: 1) that the athlete has consciously applied themselves to a given goal/goals and has recorded their success (or failure) critically; and 2) that they begin to lift their SC and self-efficacy in a step-by-step, progressive fashion.

The Competition Plan

Formulating a competition plan well in advance will prepare the athlete in a way that will boost their confidence, reduce anxiety and improve self-efficacy. This plan should be detailed and reinforce what the athlete wants to achieve. It should reflect the competitive conditions they will face. Here is a real (personal) example of what can be included:

I knew that I responded positively to competition and that I would run faster on the long jump run-up in response to other athletes jumping further. I would get increasingly motivated and my adrenaline (and mental state) would allow me to recruit more fast twitch muscle fibre, enabling me to run faster. Consequently, I would often 'no jump' as I pushed that bit harder on my approach. I realised that taking my run-up back by 20–30cm, when hyped up prior to jumping in such a situation, would prevent me from fouling and give me the best chance of achieving a winning jump.

It will take time and training maturity to develop a detailed training plan, but the process and its application are well worth it.

2: Attribution

Works on: Objectively assessing the athlete's performances and aims to put them in control of developing motivation and confidence (again, boosts self-efficacy).

Attribution should be used to PP and analyse SC goals and competitive performances. The technique is used to avoid blaming external factors for poor performance (or excellent ones). Rather, the athlete searches for the real causes of competitive success or failure.

How: The athlete needs to reflect objectively on why they were successful (or not) in a particular competition or in terms of a specific training goal. For an important competition they should not do this until the immediate emotions (such as jubilation or disappointment) have subsided. It is also best to attribute in the company of someone they can trust; someone who knows them well and who can be as objective as possible. Invariably, this should be the athlete's coach. This person should confirm or challenge the athlete's attributions. Once these have been established, the athlete can then take further mental and physical steps to control their performance outcomes. Here's an example:

Let's assume an athlete has performed below expectation because of weather conditions. It is easy to say that the wind and rain affected performance, but 'the conditions were the same for everyone'. A realistic attribution (and future goal) could be, 'I did not prepare sufficiently in similar conditions and will make sure that I do this in future. The conditions were the same for everyone'. A relevant training/competition plan should be drawn up accordingly.

So, for the above example, the athlete could mentally and physically train in different weather conditions (*see also* 'How to Develop and Improve Mental Toughness', page 179).

To reiterate, the aim of attribution is to put the athlete in control, to make them feel that they can significantly determine their own performance.

3: Visualisation

Works on: Improving all aspects of performance, conditioning-wise, technically and motivationally.

Visualisation involves the athlete 'seeing' in their mind a winning and/or technically correct performance. They may also see themselves in the optimum mental state. When they do this, electrical messages will be sent from their brain to their muscles, in much the same way as if the skill were actually being physically performed. This will teach the skills required in much the same way as physical training.

How: To get the most from visualisation the athlete needs to adopt a systematic approach (as with physical training). They should set aside a specific time and place. This 'place' should be quiet and free from distractions. To visualise, the athlete should run over in their mind, time after time, the skill, performance state or performance they wish to achieve. This should be done in various conditions, to ready the athlete for all possibilities. A sprinter, for example, could run their race from all lanes, or from the lane they know they have been drawn in for the race.

It is important that visualisations are done at real speed or faster and that they reflect real physical sporting conditions. If a sprinter visualises themselves running with perfect technique, but in slow motion, they will be patterning in a slower sprinting response.

Visualisation for Endurance Athletes

It is apparent that visualisation can work for the learning of sports skill, but can it be as useful a method for enhancing endurance or ultra perform-ance, where technique, such as running, has been mastered? Considerable research into this subject has taken place at the University of Wolverhampton. By studying the researchers' recommendations, endurance athletes and coaches will be able to see how visualisation can be applied to their disciplines.

The researchers use imagery to help athletes cope with difficult situations. They stress that it is crucial for the athlete to successfully imagine them-selves tackling a number of the factors that make the task difficult. This should never be underesti-mated; otherwise there is a risk of creating a false sense of self-confidence. Specifically, the athlete should imagine themselves coping successfully with fatigue (during the toughest part of the race). They should rehearse the psych-up strategies that would enable them to gain more energy. Self-talk (see page 179) is important in this respect, as the athlete talks their performance up and pushes the 'negative' voices away. By repeatedly applying this type of visualisation, the athlete will bolster their physical preparation for the times when the going literally gets tough. (Reference: 'Ultra-endurance psy-chology: training the mind to take control', *Peak Performance*, 2005; 226: 2–4)

For further thoughts on the role of the brain and mind on endurance performance, see pages 129–30.

Sports Training Tip

To assist the visualisation process, a sports psychol-ogist or coach can work with the athlete. They may talk to the athlete and create the right conditions for visualisation to work. They may, for example, sow the images in the athlete's mind, while the athlete relaxes with their eyes closed.

4: Getting in the Zone

Works on: Achieving optimum mental and physical condition for performance.

The 'zone of optimal functioning' (ZOF), as it is known within sports psychology, results in the optimisation of performance, as the athlete is neither too relaxed nor too psyched-up to compete. Centring (*see* below) will reduce anxiety, while energising (*see* page 179) will boost aggression, if this is needed.

While in the zone, the athlete will experi-ence what is known as a peak flow state when the task they are performing becomes easy and fluid, yet highly effective.

5: Centring

Works on: Relaxation and reducing excessive nervousness prior to competition.

Centring uses a breathing technique devel-oped by Tibetan monks over 2000 years ago. It can be used to reduce anxiety before compe-titions. Sports psychologists believe that if this skill is practised for a minute a day for two weeks, preferably in front of a mirror, the athlete will master it for life and will only need to practise it once a week thereafter to main-tain it.

How:

1 Stand with feet shoulder-width apart in front of mirror.
2 Relax the upper body, paying particular attention to neck and shoulders.
3 Focus on the movement of the abdominal muscles.
4 Breathe in slowly and deeply and 'see' the stomach extend.
5 Focus and relax. The body should feel heavier as centring is continued.

6: Energising

Works on: Increasing competitive aggression.

Sometimes an athlete can be too relaxed to be in the zone before they compete and may need to 'psych' themselves up.

How: The athlete should focus on something that will boost their arousal, such as going to fight for a worthy cause or their dislike for a certain person (or fellow competitor; you do not have to hate them afterwards!).

Use self-talk: the athlete talks themselves up into a more *fired-up* state. They should use positive statements, such as, 'I am stronger and faster than the other runners.' Note: The use of aggression-lifting techniques should be carefully monitored by coaches, particularly of team sports. Rugby players, for example, may attempt to raise their aggression before a game by aggressive practices; this can result in them entering the field of play too 'charged' and likely to perform badly and infringe, with potential match-losing consequences.

Mental Toughness

When considering the development of endurance, I noted that mental fortitude has been identified as perhaps the key factor in determining who wins and who loses, everything else being equal. In all sporting contests there is truth in the maxim that 'when the going gets tough the tough get going'. Sports psychologists specifically use the term 'mental toughness' to describe the mental qualities that enable some athletes to perform better than others.

What is Mental Toughness?

Athletes who possess mental toughness are seen to:

Focusing the Mind Can Maintain Strength and Healing Speed when Injured

More and more research is appearing that validates neural/mental factors in developing/maintaining strength and speeding up recovery after injury. For instance, various studies exist that display that:

- focusing on an injured limb can increase its rate of recovery. The athlete's focus may include visualisation of the injured part being flushed out with fresh blood and the damaged tissue being repaired;
- focusing on developing strength and power in a muscle or muscle group can actually assist strength/power development (without training);
- training an uninjured limb and focusing mentally on the other, when the other is injured, can lead to strength maintenance/less strength decline in the injured limb than when no training is performed (this is a neural response).

(See also 'Maladaptive Pain', page 157.)

- achieve consistently high performances;
- possess consistently high levels of confidence (and self-efficacy – *see* page 180);
- cope better with 'distractions', inside and outside of the sporting world;
- deal better with pain and discomfort;
- deal better with setbacks and injury.

How to Develop and Improve Mental Toughness

In terms of whether this trait is learned or present from birth (the 'nature/nurture' debate), current thinking has it that it is an amalgam of both. So, what about the nurture part? How can mental toughness be learned and developed? Here is an example that can be adapted to various sports:

Subject the Athlete to 'Controlled' Stressors

For example, a high jump athlete is performing a technique session; all is going well. The coach then decides to stop the workout for 15 minutes (a reason may or may not be given), although the athlete is told to keep warm, focused and ready to continue. This training situation will familiarise the athlete with the stop/start nature of high jump competitions and the occasional times when bad weather can hold up an event. They will develop increased confidence in dealing with these potential performance stressors when they happen for 'real'. The coach should monitor how the athlete reacts to the enforced break and then work with them to develop the best mental and physical approach to the 'wait'.

In order for this objective to be achieved fully, coach/athlete should evaluate what happened during this and other similar situations designed to develop mental toughness. From this it will be possible to develop and revise the competition plan.

Arousal

Arousal refers to the level of aggression required to achieve optimum performance readiness. Some sports benefit from greater levels of arousal than others. For example, taking a penalty in football would not benefit from the same level of arousal required of a weightlifter. Both athletes, however, still need 'control' if they are to perform their two very difficult skills as effectively as possible.

Sports Training Tip

Fast twitch muscle fibre requires greater mental input to switch it on compared to slow twitch muscle fibre. The athlete should be in the 'best' mental state to get the most from its power-producing capability. This may require mental techniques that raise their level of arousal.

Confidence/self-efficacy

Athletes with high levels of self-efficacy basically believe that they will succeed.

'Self-efficacy' is a term used within psychology; it refers to the belief that individuals have in their ability to perform a task. The concept was developed by the American psychologist, Albert Bandura, and can be applied to all aspects of life, including sporting situations. Self-efficacy beliefs determine how people feel, think, motivate themselves and behave. Athletes with high levels of self-efficacy basically believe they will be successful.

Sports Training Tip

When young athletes compete, the emphasis should be placed on personal outcomes, rather than on who actually wins and loses. The young athlete should focus on their own performance and how well they are doing 'against' themselves.

Table 9.2	**Factors that Affect Self-efficacy and Developmental Techniques**
Factors that affect self-efficacy	Developmental techniques
Performance accomplishments	Reminding the athlete of their accomplishments e.g. by video tape
Vicarious experiences – an athlete may not have performed at a venue or against certain competitors before, and may have reduced self-efficacy because of this	The athlete talks with coaches/athletes who are familiar with the impending competitive situation. Videos could be shown of similar-stature athletes, successfully performing under the 'new' competitive situation.
Verbal persuasion (from others and self)	Relatively self-explanatory, although the athlete should be positive and objective (see 'Attribution', page 177)
Psychological state – physiological signals may trigger various psychological states in the athlete, ranging from competitive readiness to anxiety	Relaxation techniques and, if necessary, arousal techniques are learned to 'control' these feelings

Skill Acquisition

Mastering sport skills is crucial if an athlete is to get as close as they can to optimising their ability. It can be incredibly frustrating for coach and athlete to know that the latter 'has the ability' but is being let down by poor technique. The roots of good sporting technique should be laid at an early age and reinforced by practice, both mental and physical. There are optimum years for skill learning, as indicated in part 1. However, this does not mean that a child should be able to perform a complex specific skill, such as a four-turn hammer throw; rather that they should be taught the basic movement patterns required for running, jumping, throwing, kicking and so on. In doing so they will develop a repertoire of skills that will enable them to perform more complex sports skills more proficiently, such as the actual hammer throw in later life, if this is their sport of choice.

Learning

Athletes learn differently. It is crucial that their coach is aware of this and does not adopt a blanket approach to skill learning, particularly in team sports. Stages of skill acquisition have been identified. These are often termed the 'understanding stage', the 'practising stage' and the 'maintaining stage'. Each of these requires a different coaching approach, summarised below:

Table 9.3	**Skill Learning Stages and Key Methods to Encourage Skill Learning**
Skill learning stage	Key methods to encourage skill learning
Understanding stage	Instruction, demonstration, analysis, questioning
Practising stage	Feedback (given and generated), questioning, listening
Maintaining stage	As above

Feedback

All of the key methods in Table 9.3 are forms of feedback. It is crucial for coaches to provide quality feedback that does not 'overload' the athlete. For example, it will be difficult for a tennis player to think of 'foot, hip, shoulder and wrist position' all at the same time in the split second they hit a top spin forehand, if instructed to do so by the coach. Rather, concentrating on an aspect of technique (as part of the whole movement) will offer greater focus. In this respect, 'associations' such as 'lift and hit' can also be useful, as long as the tennis player, in this example, knows what this means. These words should become 'triggers' that fire the technique when the athlete runs through them in their mind, or when they are communicated by the coach. (*See also* 'Skill/strength Periodisation', part 8, page 168.)

Sports Training Tip

Some athletes learn quicker than others; some will want to break down the activity into its component parts (called 'chunking') while others will prefer to learn a movement as a whole. The coach should adapt their approach accordingly.

Sports Training Tip

Be aware of the maxim 'practice makes perfect' – only 'perfect practice makes perfect'. Coach/athlete should be mindful of not patterning 'bad habits' as they can be difficult to shake off.

PART **TEN**

BOOSTING SPORTS PERFORMANCE: NUTRITION

What an athlete eats and drinks, and the supplements they take, can significantly affect their performance. Optimising nutrition for sport can boost recovery between workouts and after injury, reduce cellular damage, improve endurance potential and build more muscle. In this part I provide a practical guide on how and what an athlete should consume to achieve peak performance.

The Macronutrients

Carbohydrate, fat and protein are 'macronutrients' (vitamins and minerals are the main 'micronutrients', *see* page 196). Carbohydrate, fat and protein have very different functions in the body for general health and sports purposes. Table 10.5 (*see* page 194) identifies the energy released by macronutrients per gram (in calories). Carbohydrate and fat are the preferred energy sources during exercise, when they are broken down to produce ATP (*see* page 6). Protein can also supply energy but usually only as a result of prolonged endurance activity, when the body's stores of carbohydrate and fat are running low. Note: the use of protein as an energy source is not recommended.

Carbohydrate

Carbohydrate is the body's prime fuel source when it is physically active. When digested, carbohydrate increases blood sugar levels and provides energy through chemical reactions that occur within the muscles (*see* 'ATP' and 'Glycolysis', pages 5–6). For most athletes, carbohydrate should constitute 60 per cent of food consumption.

Simple and Complex Carbohydrates

Carbohydrates can be divided into simple (sugars, also known as monosaccharides) and complex types (fibres and starches, also known as polysaccharides). Simple carbohydrates contain one or two sugar units in their molecules, while complex carbohydrates contain from 10 to thousands of units.

When the body is at rest, carbohydrate travels via the bloodstream to the liver and skeletal muscle where it is stored as glycogen, a starch-like substance made up of numerous glucose molecules, and used to fuel exercise.

The amount of glycogen stored in the body is influenced by numerous factors, such as training status and carbohydrate consumption. About 400g of glycogen is stored in the muscles, while the liver can store about 70g. Liver glycogen plays a crucial role in providing energy for the brain (where it is received as glucose) and muscles during exercise. Failure to receive this energy source will result in a feeling of faintness and giddiness. Glycogen is also present in the blood in small amounts – about 15g – which can provide 60 Kcal of energy.

In terms of energy potential, average glycogen stores amount to 1600–2000 Kcal – this would provide enough energy for one day if a person went without food.

Glycaemic Index

Many foods contain a mixture of simple and complex carbohydrates, so to measure their immediate energy release they are given a glycaemic index (GI) rating. This ranges from 1–100. Low-GI foods release their energy more slowly than high-GI foods. Table 10.1 identifies the GI of selected foods. It is important to know the GI of foods, for general and specific sports nutrition purposes. As an example, a high-GI food/drink would make a good choice for in-race/competition fuelling for an endurance athlete, as it will provide quick energy.

An elite triathlete performing two or more training sessions a day would need 10–12g of carbohydrate per kg of body weight.

Athletes Need to Eat!

High-fat carbohydrates, such as ice cream, pastries and pizza, should be eaten sparingly to avoid unwanted weight gain. However, athletes – particularly those involved in field sports and endurance activities – can burn more than 4000 calories a day, and it is therefore possible for them not to eat enough to maintain their energy needs. This becomes even more of a potential problem when estimates of calorific requirements fail to account for training-induced increases in metabolic rate and their impact on calorific need (see page 196). Female athletes in particular need to see food as a vital fuel source and eat sufficient quantities to fuel their tank optimally. Many may be pressured to avoid eating 'too much', with negative consequences on health and performance (see page 191).

Carbohydrate Loading

Carbohydrate loading (carbo-loading) has been used since the 1960s as a nutritional strategy to enhance endurance performance lasting more than 90 minutes. The aim is to boost glycogen stores by optimising the use of carbohydrate as a fuel source. This is seen to extend endurance by increasing the ability of the body to use carbohydrate as a fuel source.

To carbo-load, the athlete should consume a high-carbohydrate diet for three days prior to a competition, while in a tapering (peaking) training phase. It is counterproductive for the athlete to train hard right up to important competitions as this will deplete glycogen stores and partially negate the benefits of carbo-loading.

With carbo-loading it is possible to increase glycogen stores by 20 per cent above normal.

Six days out from the competition, the athlete should consume 5–7g of carbohydrate per kilogram of body weight, and increase this to 8–10g in the final three days before competition.

A word of caution: always experiment with any new nutritional or training technique in training before trying it in competition.

The majority of research indicates a 20 per cent improvement in endurance as a result of carbohydrate loading.

Estimating the Energy Release of Meals

There are several factors that need to be taken into account when working out the energy release of meals:

- Protein and fat reduce GI.
- For meals that combine two different GI-rated foods in roughly the same quantity, such as rice and kidney beans, total the GI of the two foods and divide by two. For example: white rice GI = 87, kidney beans GI = 27, total GI = 114. Therefore the meal's average GI = 57 (114 divided by 2).
- The smaller the size of the food particles, the more quickly food is digested and the faster it will release energy – hence the high GI of foods like bread and breakfast cereals.

Sports Training Tip

Knowing the GI of foods will enable athlete/coach to optimise food energy. For example, if the athlete needs a quick boost, perhaps before a workout, then a high-GI food is a good choice. Low-GI foods eaten regularly throughout the day will then provide the athlete with a steady supply of energy, which will reduce (normally fat) cravings and help them control their body weight.

Table 10.1	Selected Carbohydrates and their Glycaemic Index (GI)	

	GI
Sugars	
Glucose	100
Sucrose	65
Bread, Rice and Pasta	
Rice (white)	87
Rice (brown)	76
Bread (white)	70
Bread (wholemeal)	69
Pizza	60
Breakfast Cereals	
Cornflakes	84
Weetabix	69
Muesli	56
Porridge with water	42
Fruit	
Watermelon	72
Pineapple	66
Raisins	66
Banana	55
Grapes	46
Orange	44
Plum	39
Apples	38
Vegetables	
Baked potato	85
Broad beans	79
Chips	75
Boiled potato	56
Carrots	49
Peas	48
Dairy Products	
Ice cream	61
Custard	43
Skimmed milk	32
Full-fat milk	27
Pulses	
Butter beans	31
Red kidney beans	27
Soya beans	18
Biscuits and Snacks	
Rice cakes	85
Tortillas	72
Mars bar	68
Shortbread	64
Muesli bar	61
Muffin	44
Peanuts	14

Refuelling after a Tough Workout/competition

It is crucial that the athlete begins the refuelling process as soon as possible after their workout. This will boost the replenishment of glycogen. The most effective strategy is 50g of carbohydrate every two hours, over a 20-hour period. Moderate- to high-GI carbohydrates are best used. It makes little difference whether they are fluid or solid. However, it is essential to note that protein has been identified as being equally important in the post-exercise refuelling process as carbohydrate. This is because it can kick-start the rebuilding of muscle protein that has been broken down through exercise. This is a crucial consideration for power athletes whose training and competitions will break down muscle protein, and for endurance athletes whose activity may use protein as a fuel source.

In-training/competition Carbohydrate Feeding

As well as carbo-loading, athletes who participate in competitions or workouts lasting more than 90 minutes can further defer the emptying of their glycogen tank. To achieve this, the athlete must find out what in-race/training food/drink strategy best suits them. Experiment in training, not competition. As a guide, a 70kg athlete should consume 30–60g of carbohydrate per hour, depending on competition/workout duration, and a 60kg athlete 25–50g.

In-race/competition fuelling tips:

- High-GI foods should be selected, such as energy bars or sports drinks with a 6–10 per cent carbohydrate content (*see* page 203 for more on sports drinks).
- Consuming small amounts of food and/or drink regularly during prolonged endurance activity is better tolerated by the stomach than larger quantities.
- Carbo-load before races.

Fat

Fat provides the body with energy. It is also important in terms of hormone metabolism, tissue structure and for the cushioning of other important tissue. Despite its importance, however, athletes (and non-athletes) have become particularly concerned about its consumption. Although this is warranted in some cases – as fat consumed in too great a quantity will have negative effects – overlooking the positive contribution of this food source will have just as many potentially negative consequences for athletes.

Too much body fat for most athletes serves no useful function. Simply put, it acts as added resistance for them to carry around. This increases the energy required to sustain an activity, which becomes vital in terms of winning and losing. Not surprisingly, athletes often strive for the lowest possible body fat levels. However, this is not without its dangers.

Different Types of Fat

For most athletes, fat should constitute 30 per cent of food consumption, in the proportions outlined in this section. Note: Female endurance athletes, in particular, may benefit from increasing their consumption of 'good' fat (*see* page 191).

Saturated Fat

Saturated fat should constitute less than 10 per cent of total fat consumption. Found mainly, but not exclusively, in dairy and animal products, this is the most 'harmful' type of fat, as in excess it can raise low-density lipoprotein (LDL) cholesterol*. Examples of saturated fat include butter, cheese and the fat on meat – they are all hard at room temperature.

Trans-fatty Acids

In brief, these should be treated as saturated fats and not be consumed excessively. They are the result of attempts to prolong the shelf life of monounsaturated and polyunsaturated fats, and can be found in a large number of processed foods.

Unsaturated Fats

Monounsaturated fats are found in olive oil, nuts and seeds, and can reduce LDL cholesterol and

---

* Cholesterol is a part of all cell membranes and is needed by the body. It contributes to the production of several hormones. Cholesterol is in part derived from the food we eat, but is in the main produced in the liver from saturated fats. Too much LDL cholesterol is detrimental to (heart) health.

its negative effects. These fats are normally liquid at room temperature. They should make up around 12 per cent of daily food consumption.

Polyunsaturated fats are found in most vegetable oils, oily fish, nuts and seeds. They are liquid at room temperature and below. This type of fat can also reduce LDL cholesterol. It is recommended that around 10 per cent of daily food consumption comes from these fats.

Essential Fatty Acids (Omega-3 and Omega-6 Series)

Essential fatty acids (EFAs) cannot be produced in the body and must be provided by food. They have a crucial hormone-like action, as they can regulate numerous body functions. However, modern food processing methods often result in their nutritional value being significantly reduced.

Omega-3 essential fatty acids are found in some nuts and seeds, such as flax and pumpkin seeds, walnuts, soya beans and oily fish, such as sardines, mackerel, salmon, trout and herrings. Alpha-linoleic acid is a common omega-3 fatty acid.

Omega-3 fatty acids have numerous sports-enhancing functions. They can:

- improve oxygen and nutrient transport to cells;
- improve aerobic energy metabolism;
- help prevent strain injuries as they have anti-inflammatory properties;

- benefit the immune system, thus reducing susceptibility to illness;
- increase growth hormone secretion as a consequence of sleep and/or exercise.

Omega-6 fatty acids reduce LDL cholesterol and are beneficial to the athlete mainly due to their anti-inflammatory properties.

Recommendations as to the exact amount of EFAs an athlete should consume often conflict. However, as a starting point, 9g of omega-6 and 6g of omega-3 should be aimed for each day. Table 10.2 provides information on the EFA content of selected foods.

Minimum Body Fat Levels for Athletes

To some athletes, low body fat levels are as much to trumpet about as gold medals. However, failure to understand the role of fat and the effects of too little fat can lead to impaired sports performance and health (and no gold medals!).

Male athletes can achieve a minimum body fat level as low as 5 per cent. Women can achieve minimum levels of 10 per cent. Lower values can lead to health problems for both sexes. Women may suffer from menstrual cycle irregularities (oligomenorrhoea) and cessation (amenorrhoea), infertility and reduced bone density (increasing the risk of stress fractures).

Table 10.2 The EFA Content of Selected Foods		
Food	Omega-3 per 100g	Omega-6 per 100g
Salmon	3.2	0.7
Walnuts	3.0	3.2
Butter	1.2	1.8
Olive oil	0.6	7.9
Wheat germ	0.5	5.5
Olives	0	1.6

Do Endurance Athletes Need More Fat?

The role of fat in an athlete's diet, as noted, can be undervalued. A team of researchers focused on the role that fat can play in the lives of female endurance athletes. These athletes are often on low-fat diets and may be suffering from insufficient calorific intake, which makes them susceptible to amenorrhoea (see page 190) and reduced performance potential. The researchers recommended that female endurance athletes in particular could get as much as 40 per cent of their calories from (good) fat sources. This should be seen in the context of the trained endurance athlete's body being much more effective at using fat as a fuel source compared to the untrained or non-endurance athlete. (Reference: *Sports Med.*, 2002; 32(5): 323–37)

Female endurance athletes, in particular, are prone to menstrual cycle irregularities caused by training and low body fat. It has been estimated that more than 6 out of 10 of them will suffer from this condition. Accordingly, they and other female athletes must ensure that they consume sufficient calories to sustain their energy requirements, sports performance and health (*see* page 196).

Amenorrhoea reduces the amount of the female sex hormone (oestrogen) in the body, which has numerous negative consequences, as previously noted. With dietary and training changes, the menstrual cycle will normally return within three months. It is recommended that female athletes consult a doctor if they have not had a normal period for six months.

Men may experience loss of libido and sex drive when their body fat drops to around 5 per cent. Low body fat levels for both men and women will increase the likelihood of them suffering from infections, due to reduced immune system function.

Body Fat Levels: Male and Female Athletes Compared with the 'Normal' Population

A very lean male endurance runner with 5 per cent body fat will have 3kg of fat; their female counterpart with 15 per cent body fat will have approximately 8kg of fat. Young women's 'normal' body fat ranges are between 25 and 30 per cent, and men's are between 15 and 18 per cent. From these figures it can be appreciated why sportswomen in particular see and feel the need to push their body fat below levels that their bodies were not designed to handle.

Female Athletes and Eating Disorders

Research indicates that female athletes are at risk of suffering from eating disorders. One particular study focused on 283 elite Spanish sportswomen competing in 20 different sports. Interestingly, the researchers wanted to find out whether the exposure of the athlete's body in public had any influence on attitudes to diet, in terms of public pressure and coaches' attitudes. Worryingly, it was discovered that:

- 20.14 per cent of the women surveyed probably had bulimia nervosa* (five times greater than for Spanish women of a similar age);
- skaters and gymnasts displayed a high level of eating disorders: 6 per cent fitted the criteria for anorexia nervosa** and 19.4 per cent for bulimia;
- pressure from coaches was significantly linked with the risk of bulimia.

These (and other) findings led the researchers to conclude that, 'Athletes (in certain sports)

* Bulimia nervosa refers to a cycle of eating and the forced throwing up of food.
** Anorexia nervosa is defined as a clinical condition when food consumption is severely restricted, despite the person being 15 per cent or more below ideal weight.

should be supervised clinically and . . . the conduct of their coaches and others in charge of sports activities should be monitored.'

Coaches of female athletes should therefore be aware of the potential for eating disorders. As this research indicates, they should objectively monitor their athletes' eating behaviours and, just as importantly, their attitudes to the eating and appearance of those in their charge. (Reference: *Int. J. Sports Med.*, 2005; 26: 693–700)

Fat as an Energy Source

At low to moderate aerobic exercise intensities, fat provides about 50 per cent of the energy required to fuel activity, along with carbohydrate. With increasing intensity, more carbohydrate is utilised, so that above 90 per cent of HRMax very little fat contributes to energy production. However, as noted, when considering carbohydrate (stored as muscle and liver glycogen), there are times when fat (and protein) take on a key role in furnishing further energy for the endurance athlete. This occurs when glycogen stores have been depleted, normally after 90–180 minutes of exercise, or at intensities that enable fat to supply most of the body's energy.

Endurance athletes can improve their body's ability to use fat as an energy source. Base-building aerobic training (*see* page 114) increases the number of their fat-oxidising enzymes, such as lipoprotein lipase, which creates more usable fat as fuel (as fatty acids) in the muscular furnaces. The number of mitochondria (cellular power plants) can also be increased as a result of endurance training, thus increasing energy creation and fat utilisation potential. Greater numbers of capillaries will also boost fat-burning as a fuel source, as they allow greater quantities of fatty acids to reach the muscles to be used as fuel. All these factors can significantly increase the endurance athlete's ability to use fat and increase their endurance potential.

Exercise scientists have coined the term 'fat max' to describe the exercise intensity at which fat supplies an optimal supply of energy. This is difficult to work out outside laboratory conditions, but can be as high as 85 per cent of HRMax in the supremely conditioned endurance athlete. (*See* part 6, page 122 for further information on fat max and fat as a fuel source.)

Table 10.3	Selected Sports and Average Body Fat Levels (%)	
Sport	Men	Women
Basketball	7–12	18–27
Football	8–18	N/A
Gymnastics	4–6	8–18
Running	4–12	8–18
Tennis	12–16	22–26
Weightlifting	6–16	17–20

Adapted from A. Bean, *The Complete Guide to Sports Nutrition* (third edition), p. 98, A&C Black, 2002

Protein

Protein constitutes about 20 per cent of the body's weight. It is a part of every tissue and cell in the body, including muscle, hair, internal organs, skin and nails. Protein is involved in producing hormones and enzymes. It also has a role in optimising tissue fluid balance and transporting nutrients to and from cells. For sports training purposes, protein is needed to repair and develop muscle tissue that has been broken down through training. In these circumstances, it acts as a building block. As noted previously, protein can also supply energy, but only under prolonged endurance conditions.

As noted, protein should constitute about 20 per cent of food consumption. However, this has not stopped athletes (and the general population) experimenting with higher-protein diets.

How Much Protein? Aerobic/Endurance versus Anaerobic/Power Athletes

Most research indicates that too much protein consumption will have no positive effect on the body. In fact, like any food consumed in too great a quantity, it will either be excreted from the body or turned to fat. Consequently, it is generally accepted that 1.8–2g of protein per kilogram of body weight is the maximum amount that a strength/power athlete, such as a high jumper or weightlifter, should consume per day. Endurance athletes should ensure a daily protein intake of at least 1.6g per kilogram of body weight. Note: If the latter perform more regular resistance work, such as weight-training, plyometrics and circuit training, and are undertaking numerous long efforts in training (such as runs of over 16 miles), then increasing their protein consumption to the limit previously identified should be considered.

Endurance athletes should also be aware of the catabolic effect of their training, particularly when it is regular and prolonged.

Protein and Recovery

Protein consumption post- (and pre-) workout may be as important as carbohydrate consumption in terms of speeding up and optimising recovery and maximising training gains, hence the use of carbohydrate/protein-based recovery drinks.

Rather like carbohydrate and GI, proteins vary in their rate of assimilation into the body. There are actually 'fast' and 'slow' proteins – the speed refers to the rate at which they release their amino acid content.

Whey is the most quickly absorbed protein in sports drinks, taking about two hours to release its amino acid content. Other commonly used proteins in sports drinks include casein, egg and soy – their rate of amino acid release varies between five and seven hours.

Amino Acids

Amino acids are protein building blocks. There are eight *essential* amino acids, which cannot be synthesised in the body, and 12 *non-essential* amino acids, which can be made in the body, provided enough of the essential amino acids are present. Table 10.4 identifies the essential and non-essential amino acids.

During endurance activities lasting more than an hour, specific amino acids (valine, leucine and isoleucine) in muscles are used as a fuel source, as glycogen stores deplete. At this time, protein can supply 15 per cent of the body's energy requirements, compared to its normal 5 per cent when glycogen stores are full. As noted, training at fat max regularly will offset protein and carbohydrate usage in endurance activities.

After weight and other power training workouts, such as plyometric ones, protein is needed to boost muscle growth during rest and recovery. In order to achieve this, more protein must be consumed than is broken down and/or used as energy. As noted, this should be 1.6–2 per kilogram of body weight a day (*see also* 'Sports Drinks', page 203).

Table 10.4	Essential and Non-essential Amino Acids	
Essential amino acids	**Non-essential amino acids**
Isoleucine	Alanine
Leucine	Arginine
Lysine	Asparagine
Methionine	Aspartic acid
Phenylalanine	Cysteine
Theronine	Glutamic acid
Tryplophan	Glutamine
Valine	Glycine
	Histidine (essential for babies only)
	Proline
	Serine
	Tyrosine

Adapted from A. Bean, *The Complete Guide to Sports Nutrition*, third edition, p. 33, A&C Black, 2002

How to Calculate an Athlete's Calorific Requirements

In this section I provide information that will enable coach/athlete to calculate energy expenditure, and therefore dietary needs. Metabolism (and its variations) will also be explained accordingly.

Step 1: Calculate Resting Metabolic Rate (RMR)

Abbreviations and Definitions

RMR = resting metabolic rate, referencing essential bodily functions such as heart, lung and mental functioning
TDEE = total daily energy expenditure, the energy used day and night to maintain life

A very significant proportion (60–75 per cent) of TDEE is used to maintain RMR. Calculations of RMR are made over a 24-hour period but do not include the calories used while sleeping. (*See* page 196 for a focus on the effects of intense training on metabolic rate.)

Understanding Food Energy

Metric: 1Kcal = 1000 cal
Imperial: 1 calorie = 1000 c
A *Kcal* and a *calorie* supply the same amount of energy (that is why the terms can be used interchangeably).

1 cal is the amount of heat required to increase the temperature of 1 gram (g) of water by 1 degree centigrade. It is a very small amount of energy, hence the general use of the bigger Kcal unit.

The *Kilojoule* is the international standard for energy: 1 kJ = 1000 j. A kJ is not the same as a Kcal (or calorie) in terms of its energy provision. kJ can be converted into Kcal and vice versa by using the following calculations:

- To convert kJ into Kcal divide by 4.2, thus 200kJ = 48 Kcal (200/4.2)
- To convert Kcal into kJ multiply by 4.2, thus 100 Kcal = 420 kJ (100 × 4.2)

Table 10.5	Energy Release from Different Macronutrients		
Macronutrient	Carbohydrate	Protein	Fat
Energy in Kcal/g	4	4	9

Table 10.6	How to Calculate RMR	
Age	Male	Female
10–18	Body weight in kg × 17.5 + 651	Body weight in kg × 12.2 + 746
18–30	Body weight in kg × 15.3 + 679	Body weight in kg × 14.7 + 496
31–60	Body weight in kg × 11.6 + 879	Body weight in kg × 8.7 + 829

65kg male age 18–30
65kg × 15.3 + 679
RMR = 1673.5

65kg female age 31–60
65kg × 8.7 + 829
RMR =1394.5

80kg male age 18–30
80kg × 15.3 +
679 RMR = 1903

60kg female age 10–18
60kg × 12.2 +
746 RMR = 1478

Thermic Effect of Feeding

About 10 per cent of TDEE is used to digest and process food. This is known as the 'thermic effect of feeding' (TEF). Athlete/coach may be surprised to hear that sports training (and other activity) accounts for only around 15 per cent of TDEE. However, this and its long-term effects, in terms of constantly increasing metabolic rate, have a very significant influence on energy and calorific balance.

Step 2: Estimate the Athlete's Daily Activity Requirements in Calories

Multiply RMR by daily activity level according to the relevant number below:

Table 10.8	Daily Activity Levels	
Activity level	Defined as	
Not training	Some physical activity, perhaps at work or as active recovery at end of training year	RMR × 1.7
In training	Regular sports workouts	RMR × 2.0

Selected examples:
18–30 year-old male, 80kg, 'in training': 1903 x 2.0 = 3806 Kcal
31–60 year-old female, 60kg, 'not training': 1478 x 1.7 = 2512 Kcal

Adapted from A. Bean, *The Complete Guide to Sports Nutrition*, third edition, pp. 112–113, A&C Black, 2002

The Effects of Sports Training on Metabolic Rate

Although athlete/coach may carefully calculate the number of calories that the former needs for their respective sports activities (using the equations provided), they may actually under-estimate true calorific requirements by as much as 20 per cent. Neglected factors include:

- a consistently elevated metabolic rate resulting from regular training that can increase calorific expenditure by as much as 17 per cent;
- the metabolic cost of lean muscle, which can burn up to three times more calories than non-lean body tissue – a 0.5kg gain in muscle can increase weekly calorie burn by 350 Kcal.

The elevation in RMR as a consequence of training is specifically known as 'excess post-exercise oxygen consumption' (EPOC). EPOC appears to have two phases: one lasting less than two hours and one that has a more prolonged effect, lasting up to 48 hours. The former is seen to be more significant in terms of calorie burning than the latter.

EPOC and Different Sports

The mechanisms underlying short-term EPOC created by endurance training are well known. They involve the following bodily processes:

- The replenishment of oxygen stores
- Adenosine triphosphate/creatine phosphate re-synthesis
- Lactate removal
- Increased body temperature, circulation and ventilation

However, those applicable to the longer lasting EPOC are less well known, although a sustained increase in circulation, ventilation and body temperature may contribute. Interestingly, little is known about the mechanisms underlying EPOC after resistance exercise.

Athlete/coach must be mindful of the implications of hard training on EPOC (metabolic rate), which can leave calorie intake calculations short. As stressed, endurance athletes and, in particular, females may need to increase their fat consumption in order to maintain energy levels, bolster their immune system and attempt to reduce some of the problems associated with training-induced menstrual cycle irregularities. All endurance athletes should watch out, paradoxically, for metabolic slowdown as a consequence of their tough training regimes. Simply put, they may fail to consume sufficient food to maintain their 'excessive' energy expenditure, resulting in their bodies 'hanging' on to the 'insufficient' calories they get. This is similar to what happens to a person who is attempting to lose weight and cuts back drastically on calorie consumption. They end up slowing their metabolism down and gaining weight quite easily when calorie restriction is ceased. For an athlete, insufficient calorific consumption can impair performance for the numerous reasons indicated, and may also make them prone to weight fluctuations.

> Everything else being equal, the athlete who eats the most sensibly and trains the hardest will have the most consistent metabolic rate and optimum nutrition for their sport activity.

Micronutrients: Vitamins, Minerals and Antioxidants

Vitamins

Vitamins are crucial in facilitating energy release from food, but do not produce energy themselves. As with minerals, consuming excess amounts of vitamins (above recommended levels/reference nutrient intake) will not enhance their metabolic contribution.

Minerals

Twenty-two mainly metallic minerals make up 4 per cent of body mass. Their main function is to balance and regulate internal chemistry, such as the maintenance of muscular contractions, the regulation of heart beat and nerve conduction.

Antioxidants

Antioxidants include the vitamins A, C, E and betacarotene and the mineral selenium. A diet rich in antioxidants will prevent free radical damage to cells, reduce LDL cholesterol and defend the body against age-related diseases, such as cancer and heart disease.

Antioxidants are especially important for hard-training athletes, particularly those involved in endurance activities. This is because this type of training can increase free radical cellular damage. Oxygen fuels the heart and lungs and all bodily processes, including the energy release from food. Unfortunately, oxygen metabolism can create unstable molecular fragments, which can damage cells if left unchecked. Antioxidant vitamins, minerals and phytochemicals (which include bioflavonoids, *see* page 199) can combat this cellular damage.

See Tables 10.9 and 10.10 for more details of phytochemicals and other selected sports performance-enhancing vitamins and minerals.

Sports Training Tip

To ensure a plentiful supply of antioxidants and phytochemicals in their diets, athletes should eat a variety of plant foods, wholegrain rice, bread, pasta and seven to eight daily servings of fruit and vegetables.

Sports Training Tip

When considering a general multivitamin supplement, perhaps to ensure a rich antioxidant supply, bear in mind that a well-formulated supplement should contain:

- between 100–1000 per cent of the recommended daily allowance (RDA) for vitamins (but below the safe limit);
- no more than 100 per cent of the RDA for minerals.

(Reference: A. Bean, *The Complete Guide to Sports Nutrition*, third edition, A&C Black, 2002)

Table 10.9	The Positive Sports (and Health) Benefits of Selected Phytochemicals	
Phytochemical	**Source**	**Health benefits**
Allium compounds	Onions, garlic, chives, shallots	Can combat cancer and boost the immune system
Bioflavonoids	Rosehips, citrus fruits, berries, grapes, tea, red wine	Antioxidant and anti-inflammatory. Can also act as an antibiotic

Table 10.10	Vitamins and Minerals and their Specific Sports-enhancing Roles		
Vitamin/Mineral	Function	Reference Nutrient Intake (RNI)*	Selected Sources
Biotin (vitamin)	Assists glycogen manufacture and protein metabolism for muscle building	No UK RNI, 10–200ug/day is recommended	Egg yolk, nuts, oats and whole grains
Calcium (mineral)	Assists muscle contraction, hormonal signalling	Men: 1000mg/day Women: 700mg/day	Dairy products, seafood, vegetables, flour, bread, pulses
Iron (mineral)	Can assist aerobic exercise by promoting haemoglobin production of oxygen-carrying red blood cells	Men: 8.7mg/day Women: 14.8mg/day	Liver, red meat, pasta and cereals, green leafy vegetables, eggs, prunes
Zinc (mineral)	Important for metabolising proteins, carbohydrates and fats	Men: 9.5mg/day Women: 7mg/day	Lean meat and fish, eggs, wholegrain cereals, dairy products, wholemeal breads and cereals
Magnesium (mineral)	Boosts energy production and assists muscle contraction, plays a role in blood sugar stabilisation, which assists the balancing of energy levels	Men: 300 mg/day Women: 270 mg/day (Current research indicates that these figures may need increasing)	Green leafy vegetables, fruit, unrefined whole grains and wholegrain cereals
Zinc (mineral)	Zinc is an antioxidant. It also serves to activate numerous enzymes in the body that process amino acids (boosting protein synthesis), repairing and creating muscle). (Note: Recent research indicates that zinc can be beneficial to aerobic performance**.)	Men: 9.5mg/day Women: 7mg/day	Oysters, lean beef, pumpkin seeds, peanuts, turkey, wholemeal bread and flour
Copper (mineral)	Assists with collagen	1.2mg/day	Beef, liver, oysters, lamb,

Table 10.10	Vitamins and Minerals and their Specific Sports-enhancing Roles cont.		
	formation and plays an antioxidant role		peanuts, baked beans, chickpeas, wholemeal bread and wholegrain cereals
C (vitamin)	Antioxidant Assists cellular growth and repair	40mg	Fruit and vegetables, especially strawberries, oranges, tomatoes, green peppers, baked potatoes

* RNI refers to the nutrient needs of some 97 per cent of the population. For further information on RNIs, check out the British Nutrition Society at http://www.nutrition.org.uk or the English Institute of Sport at http://www.eis2win.co.uk.
** *American Journal of Clinical Nutrition*, 2005; 81: 1045–1051

Nutritional Strategies to Combat Training-induced Soft Tissue and Cellular Damage

Although understanding of the energy-producing role of food is perhaps at an all-time high, less is probably understood regarding the role of nutrition in reducing injuries and enhancing recovery.

Vitamin C

Vitamin C plays a crucial role in the formation of collagen, a protein that forms the basis for connective tissue. Specifically, vitamin C acts as a catalyst that stimulates other body chemicals to construct collagen. Vitamin C is also an antioxidant (*see* page 197).

Vitamin C is found in citrus fruits, green peppers, leafy dark green vegetables and strawberries.

Omega-3 and Omega-6 Fatty Acids

(*See* page 190.)

Bioflavonoids

Bioflavonoids have an anti-inflammatory role. Found in brightly coloured fruits and vegetables, they are part of a group of nutrients called phytochemicals. Athlete/coach may have heard of these from the recommendation that a daily glass of red wine is good for health; this is partly because of its bioflavonoid content. Bioflavonoids are also antioxidants. (*See* Table 10.9 for positive sports and health benefits of selected phytochemicals. *See also* page 200 for the use of glucosamine sulphate and chondroitin in combating soft tissue damage.)

Sports Training Tip

To ensure the athlete is adequately hydrated, they should drink enough to urinate every three to four hours. The urine should be a light colour (not dark and concentrated) and odourless.

Supplements

Nearly all athletes take supplements, sometimes in spite of sports governing bodies' recommendations and the risk of falling foul of doping legislation. It is beyond the scope of this book to go into detail about all the supplements and supplementation strategies available to the athlete and their coach. Therefore I have decided to focus on some of the more common supplements, such as creatine and glucosamine sulphate. I would also like to stress that supplements are just that – they should not be seen as substitutes for a nutritionally rich, planned and balanced natural diet. An overemphasis on supplements may result in a low-nutrient diet, which could create immune system deficiency and less (not greater) potential for positive adaptation to the stressors of prolonged and intense training.

Supplements and the Risk of Accidental Doping

Research indicates that athletes are often uneducated about the potential dangers of accidental doping. From a study of 196 Olympic level athletes from various sports, it was discovered that 5 per cent had taken a banned substance unknowingly. In conclusion, it was recommended that 'athlete-safe labelling' be used on supplements and medicinal products, and that information on supplements and doping must be improved for athletes on a 24-hour worldwide basis. (Reference: *Br. J. Sports Med.*, 2005; 39: 512–516)

Glucosamine Sulphate and Chondroitin Supplementation

Increasing research indicates that the use of the supplements glucosamine sulphate and chondroitin can reduce joint and soft tissue damage.

Glucosamine is used in the manufacture of very large molecules found in joint cartilage. These basically hold on to water, rather like a sponge, and in doing so provide cushioning for joints.

Research indicates that chondroitin heads straight to the joints and lumbar discs when ingested. Surveys, although more limited in extent when compared with glucosamine, also indicate that it reduces pain and increases mobility.

To build up *working* chondroitin and glucosamine levels in the body, try a combined supplement, ingesting 1500mg daily.

Benefits of Long-term Glucosamine Use

One clinical study, although not dealing specifically with sports participants, makes for very positive reading. It addressed the long-term effects of glucosamine sulphate supplementation on knee osteoarthritis over three years and involved 212 patients with a mean age of 66. Half took 1500mg of oral glucosamine sulphate daily, and the other half a placebo. X-rays were used to measure joint space and pain. Joint functioning, stiffness and numbers of painkillers used were also accounted for. The researchers discovered that those who supplemented suffered from no further knee joint cartilage narrowing, while the placebo group experienced a 0.5mm narrowing. On the other markers, the glucosamine group also benefited from a 20–25 per cent reduction in pain and the same increase in joint functioning. (Reference: *Lancet*, 2001; 357: 251–256)

It is recommended that coaches encourage their athletes in hard long-term training to supplement with glucosamine and/or chondroitin, perhaps from a relatively early age. It should be noted that it takes time for these supplements to start working in the body (up to six weeks in terms of pain relief) and that their effect on improving joint health requires continued use.

Creatine

Creatine has become the 'wonder' supplement, praised for its ability to benefit, in particular, speed and power athletes. Obtainable from food sources, it can also be made in the body from three amino acids. It is stored mainly as creatine phosphate (CP) in muscles. This high-energy phosphate is used to produce high-powered energy (*see* part 1, page 7).

Creatine supplementation increases CP stores in muscles by 10–40 per cent (on average by 20 per cent). Creatine's contribution to sports performance includes the following:

- It can boost anaerobic energy, making possible more repeated short-term power/speed efforts.
- It assists the development of lean muscle mass (by permitting greater training levels). The leaner the athlete, the better able they will be to burn fat due to the enhanced metabolic properties of muscle (*see* page 190 for the problems associated with too low levels of body fat).
- It boosts recovery, as muscles' creatine stores will be better maintained.

How to Get the Best Results from Creatine

To start reaping the benefits of creatine, a loading period is normally recommended. This is achieved by taking four doses of 5g per day for five days. After this, a maintenance routine is followed, normally 2g a day for four weeks. Once muscles have received their fill of creatine, further loading will provide no benefit.

Consequently, most creatine users rotate their use of this supplement, coming on and off it on a four- or five-week basis. It should be noted that when supplementation is stopped the body will continue to produce its own creatine.

At the time of writing, no major side-effects of creatine supplementation have been identified. A number of athletes do report higher levels of cramping, however, and to combat this it is crucial to remain hydrated.

Natural Sources of Creatine

Creatine is found naturally in herrings, beef, tuna, pork, salmon, milk and prawns. Note: Diet alone cannot 'creatine load' to the extent that supplementation can; although it could make a significant contribution to the 2g per day maintenance dose.

Other Potential Sports-enhancing Supplements

Glutamine: Found in muscle cells and made from three amino acids (glutamic acid, valine and isoleucine). It is essential for cell growth and immune system function. It is argued that supplementing with glutamine will:

- boost muscle recovery during periods of heavy training;
- increase immune system function.

Supplementation recommendations: 2–3g per day. It should be noted that about 50 per cent of the glutamic acid in protein supplements will be glutamine.

HMB (beta-hydroxy beta menthybutrate): Advocates of HMB supplementation believe that it will:

- increase muscle mass and reduce body fat, probably because it is involved in cellular repair;
- reduce muscle damage.

Supplementation recommendations: men: 3g per day; women: 2g per day

Hydration

Dehydration can significantly affect sporting performance. It results from inadequate fluid consumption and sweating. Exercise, particularly of high intensity and long duration in hot conditions, can lead to heat illness and, in the worst case scenario, circulatory collapse.

Specific effects of dehydration on sports performance:

- A 3–5 per cent loss in body weight caused by dehydration can significantly impair judgement, mental sharpness and reaction time.
- A 50 per cent drop in aerobic performance may result (due to decreased VO2max).
- A loss of just 2 per cent (1.5kg for an athlete weighing 75kg) in body weight caused by dehydration could impair aerobic performance by 10–20 per cent. A 4 per cent loss could result in nausea, vomiting and diarrhoea. Fluid losses greater than 5 per cent can have very significant effects on the athlete's health.

The Case for Specific Athlete Hydration

Following an analysis of the hydration practices of British professional football players, researchers from Loughborough University recommended that players should drink enough to limit weight loss to 1–3 per cent of their pre-training session/match weight. Since it is believed that salt loss can make players more prone to cramping, it was also recommended that players with a tendency to cramp should consider taking salt supplements to replace lost electrolytes.

Sweat loss during the session was measured by changes in body mass after taking account of fluids ingested in drink and excreted in urine.

Sweat composition was analysed by patches attached to the skin at four sites. On the day of testing, the weather was warm (24–29°C) with moderate humidity (46–64 per cent). Over the course of the training session, the mean body mass loss was 1.10kg, equivalent to 1.37 per cent of pre-training body mass. Mean fluid intake was 971ml, and estimated mean sweat loss was 2033ml, with a total sweat sodium loss of 99mmol, corresponding to a salt (sodium chloride) loss of 5.8g. (Reference: *Int. J. Sport Nutr. Exerc. Metab.*, 2004 Jun; 14(3): 333–46)

The implications of this research are that coaches should calculate individual athletes' hydration needs (*see* below).

Calculating Individual Athletes' Hydration Needs

As a guide, athletes should drink just enough to ensure that they lose no more than about 1–3 per cent of pre-competition weight. This can be achieved in the following way:

1 The athlete should record their naked body weight immediately before and after a number of training sessions, along with details of distance/duration, clothing and weather conditions.
2 Add drink taken during the session to weight loss, ideally working in kilograms and litres, since 1kg of weight is roughly equivalent to 1 litre of fluid.
3 After a few weeks the coach/athlete should begin to see some patterns emerging and will be able to calculate sweat rate per hour. This may be as little as 200–300ml or as much as 2–3 litres, depending on the athlete's physiology, exercise intensity, clothing and conditions.
4 Once the athlete knows their sweat loss rates applicable to particular conditions, they can plan their drinking strategy for any given event.

What and When to Drink

Having identified how to calculate fluid (sweat) loss and the importance of hydration for optimising sports performance, I will now provide information on how to maximise hydration for performance.

First, the athlete should not arrive at a training session or a competition in a dehydrated state. Drinking a sports drink with carbohydrate content (*see* Table 10.11) will prepare the body for competition and training, although water will probably be adequate in activities lasting under an hour. The athlete should aim for around 500ml of fluid two hours before exercise and an additional 125–250ml immediately prior to exercise (American College of Sports Medicine recommendations). Once exercise is started, the key is to minimise fluid loss through sweating and provide (in activities lasting longer than 60 minutes) an increase in muscle fuel (carbohydrate) to extend endurance performance. To do this, it is recommended that the athlete drink as often and as regularly as they can, aiming for 125–150ml every 10–20 minutes.

Table 10.11	Different Sports Drinks
Type of sports drink	**Constitution**
Hypotonic (fluid replacement) drink	Contains fewer particles of carbohydrate and electrolytes per 100ml than body fluid (osmolality). A hypotonic drink contains less than 4g carbohydrate/100ml, which allows it to be absorbed faster than water.
Isotonic (fluid/carbohydrate replacement) drink	Isotonic drinks have the same osmolality as body fluids, including water, and thus are absorbed at a similar rate (or faster) than water. Carbohydrate content is 4–8g/100ml.
Hypertonic (carbohydrate/energy replacement) drink	Hypertonic drinks have a higher osmolality than body fluids and are thus absorbed more slowly. Carbohydrate content is 8g/100ml. In the light of research indicating the importance of protein for recovery, a drink containing amino acids would also be highly beneficial. Minerals and vitamins contained in these drinks increase carbohydrate and protein metabolism. These drinks are better suited to aiding post-workout/competition recovery.

Note: Ordinary drinks, such as fruit juices, are not suitable for use as sports drinks as they contain 11–13g of carbohydrate and will not easily be absorbed into the body.

Electrolytes

Electrolytes are mineral salts (sodium, chloride, potassium and magnesium), which are present in bodily fluids. They regulate the fluid balance between different body compartments and the amount of fluid in the bloodstream. As an example, high cellular potassium levels increase the amount of water being pulled across a cell membrane, thus increasing the cell's water content. Although sports drinks containing electrolytes have no direct effect on performance, sodium encourages the athlete's thirst mechanism to want to drink more (plain water or sports drinks without electrolytes will not do this). This will assist them to hydrate their bodies optimally. Plain water, for example, may provide the athlete with a 'false reading' – they may think they do not need to drink any more, when in reality they do.

Post-exercise Fluid Replacement

Athletes should aim to gradually replenish 150 per cent of the fluids lost during exercise. To do this, the athlete should weigh themselves before and after their activity. To calculate how much fluid they need, they should work on the basis that 1 litre of fluid is approximately equivalent to 1 kilogram in body weight.

Sports Training Tip

For every 1000 calories of total daily energy expenditure, 1 litre of water should be consumed. Thus, 3000 calories require 3 litres of fluids; 4500 calories require 4.5 litres and so on.

Glycerol – a Means to Increase Hydration for Endurance Athletes?

Although it is not possible to 'fluid load' in the same way that athletes can carbo-load before endurance activity, glycerol offers some potential (although current sports science has yet to decide fully on its merits). Glycerol is produced naturally in the body, in consequence of normal metabolism. It is actually classed as an alcohol. The theory behind glycerol benefiting endurance athletes has it that it allows the athlete's body to hang on to greater water content. In fact, it has been argued that 'glycerol loading' can increase the induced hyper-hydrated state by up to four hours.

Some research, at the time of writing, indicates that glycerol could be beneficial for athletes competing in endurance activities in hot and humid conditions. However, under other conditions it is not worth taking. It is also recommended that glycerol drinks should be tried only once all other 'tried and tested' hydration strategies have been attempted. Do not try without experimenting in training first.

Sports Training Tip

Athletes should not fall into the trap of not drinking prior to and during training/competition in cool weather. Sweat losses can be as significant in these conditions as in hot conditions. The athlete should work out their specific hydration needs for the event, its duration and its climatic conditions (see page 202).

PART **ELEVEN**

EFFECTIVE COACHING

All the technical knowledge in the world relating to a particular sport or event does not make for a 'good' or effective coach. Although possession of knowledge will be highly beneficial, the coach still needs social and communicative skills to gain the continued trust of their athlete/athletes. Neither athlete nor coach is a machine – both will be affected by a myriad of factors from inside and outside the world of sport. It is how these 'pressures' are dealt with – and the imparting of technical knowledge – that makes for the most effective coaching.

This part should be read in conjunction with part 9, 'Training the Mind', as the coach will need to know how to maximise athletes' mental preparation.

Coaching Styles

Anyone who has attended management training (in any field) will probably be familiar with 'management/leadership styles' and 'ways of managing', for example: laissez faire, autocratic, democratic, negotiation, counsellor, teacher and charismatic roles/types/methods. Most of us will have personalities/skills that are an amalgam of aspects of each, which would make up our own coaching style. The most successful coaches are those who are able to adapt and make the 'best' behaviour choices at the 'right' times. Here's an example.

While most of us would probably reject outright the notion of being an autocratic coach, there are times when this style may be necessary. For example, when compelling an athlete mature in training years to perform one more repetition at the correct intensity, or perhaps even more poignantly, telling them when to stop when they have done enough in a workout.

The demands of professional team sports may require more autocratic leadership styles compared to other sports such as track and field and tennis. Having said this, a good football coach/manager, for example, will know which players respond more to autocratic treatment and which benefit more from a counselling approach.

Sports Training Tip

Like it or not, coaches are role models. Athletes will learn from them consciously and subconsciously. A coach must be aware of this and endeavour to be as positive and responsible as possible (see part 10, page 191 for comment on the negative impact coaches can have on female athletes and eating disorders).

Self-reflection

In order to progress, the coach needs to reflect continually, not only on which technical or conditioning aspects are working but also on their own personal effectiveness. It is key that the coach regularly evaluates their approach, ability and coaching strategy/strategies. This process will put them in the best position to get their 'coaching message' across.

To appraise coaching style more fully, the coach should consider how they coach against the coaching aspects and their associated definers (see Table 11.1). Here's what to do. Take each of the coaching definers for each coaching aspect and give each a mark out of five, using

Table 11.1	Coaching Aspects and Coaching Definers
Coaching aspect	Coaching definers
Managing	Organising, controlling, planning, timing, delegating, safeguarding, setting up, disciplining
Teaching	Facilitating, demonstrating, questioning, informing, challenging, feeding back, observing, analysing, appraising, criticising, monitoring
Communicating	Socialising, enquiring, listening, praising, supporting, planning, reading, learning, chatting, caring. Note: Communication can also be non-verbal.

Adapted from UK Athletics coaching materials

the continuum below. This process will develop a reflective, more objective appreciation of coaching style. If possible, the coach should get one or more of their athletes to complete the exercise as well; discrepancies, if any, will be well worth looking into as they may identify areas that need to be worked on. It is possible that there could be conflicting perceptions between what the coach thinks they are doing and what the athlete thinks the coach is doing.

Selected Analysis of Coaching Style Continuum

Coaching aspect: *teaching*

Coaching definer: *feedback (is provided)*
rarely not very often often very often high

  1   2   3   (4)   5

Coaching definer: *criticising (is provided)*
rarely not very often often very often high

  1   2   (3)   4   5

The examples provided should enable the coach to see how self-analysis can work. 'Our' coach provides feedback 'very often' and criticises their athletes 'often'. With reflection, this may breed a negative culture in the athletes they coach. This is because feedback may be provided negatively, with the athlete building up resentment as a consequence. In terms of a solution, the coach should try to impart feedback positively by focusing more on what 'went right' rather than on what 'went wrong'.

Self-reflection in Different Situations

Coaching does not take place in the same situation all the time. Therefore, it is very important to be honest when performing this analysis, and to analyse different responses to different situations.

Here's an example: a football manager, perhaps at the professional level, may well criticise their players to a great extent, although they may not always be fully aware of it. Consider half-time team talks, which are often highly emotional affairs where criticism is thrown around. It may be necessary for football coaches (and coaches in certain sports) to evaluate themselves in different coaching contexts as this may affect their behaviour. For example, our football manger may be much calmer on the training ground or after the team has won!

Once a coach has gained a more analytical angle on their coaching style, they need to take time out to consider whether or not they need to adapt any aspects of it (and the answer to this should nearly always be a 'yes'). It could be that they realise they are not being as effective as possible and need to work on aspects of their style. I have provided some pointers for selected scenarios below.

Improving Coaching Style and Effectiveness

Managing

The coach feels they lack control over their training sessions. Possible solutions:

- The coach may need to plan better.
- A fair rewards (and discipline) strategy may be needed to improve athletes' motivation.
- The coach may benefit from enlisting the help of a senior athlete or parent to support the athletes in training.
- The coach may simply have too many athletes in their training group and may need to reduce numbers or work with other coaches.

Teaching

The coach feels that their feedback is not as effective as it could be. Possible solutions:

- The coach may need to expand their technical knowledge.
- The coach may need to make use of video recording equipment, so that they and the athletes can immediately consider technical details.
- The coach may need to develop a greater understanding of how to give feedback to athletes – how to be precise and positive, how to reinforce and avoid information overload.

Communication

The coach may feel they need to improve their listening skills. Possible solutions:

- The coach should try not to interrupt the athlete unless they are losing focus on the skill/conditioning drill/event/performance they are talking about.
- The coach should combine listening with looking – reference the tone being used by the athlete and/or their body language.
- The coach should use objective feedback measures in order to be realistic when the athlete is describing, for example, how they felt after a competition (*see* 'Attribution', part 9, page 177).

Coaching Philosophy – Art or Science?

Coaching philosophy centres on whether coaching is art or science. As indicated previously, technical and sport-specific coaching knowledge is just one part of being a successful coach. Knowing how to blend this practical

knowledge with the specific needs of the individual/team being coached, while blending this with the coach's own style, is the art.

When coaching, we are obviously dealing with humans, not machines, so there is always going to be some degree of unpredictability. Some athletes will respond better to one type of training than others, perhaps simply because they believe in it. Other athletes will work harder for one coach than another because they respect that coach more, or they may like or even fear them. And herein lies the paradox and beauty of successful coaching as an art form: a coach may make a winner or get an athlete to achieve a personal best performance (whatever their level) against conventional wisdom. They may see something in an athlete that another coach does not.

Consequently, most coaches believe that they must be both scientist and artist in order to achieve peak performance in those they coach.

Positive Approaches for Coaching Children

In this short section I introduce some of the pitfalls and potentialities of working with young athletes and children, an area on which many coaches focus.

'The aim must be to work from success, from things that children can actually do,' says former national athletics coach, Tom McNab. Failure to adopt such an approach with young people (and adults) will reduce their self-esteem and may even lead to them dropping out of sport. From a practical standpoint, McNab suggests coaching practices that allow children to enjoy as they achieve.

How to Coach Technically

To this must be added what is said to the young athlete. For example, adopting an overly critical approach – even if not intended – when teaching a difficult sports skill can lead to feelings of low self-esteem (*see* 'Self-reflection', page 208). The coach should therefore endeavour to empower children through coaching practices designed to create an environment for the development of increasing positive self-esteem in children and young athletes (obviously, the same applies to adults).

Competition, Success and Failure

Competition can be a contentious area when coaching young athletes. The way this is introduced to young people will have a crucial effect on their psychology. Take young athletes' track and field meetings, where events will often be won by the biggest athletes, not necessarily those with the most talent. As indicated in part 1, long-term athletic development is crucial. Exposure to defeats at an early age can lead to negative self-esteem and self-efficacy (*see* page 180). It should also be noted that the young athlete who is always a winner (because they are more mature than their rivals) may also develop psychological/competition problems as they move through the age groups and their peers catch up physically and eventually begin to beat them. These athletes will not be familiar with losing and may be ill-prepared when it happens.

It is crucial that coaches control competition so that athletes learn to compete but do not become afraid of doing so or lost to sport because of it. If possible, young athletes should be encouraged to compete against themselves, to better their performances, rather than trying to beat each other. Thus, achieving a best time will reinforce confidence and boost self-efficacy. (Reference: *The Coach*, 20; Sep/Oct; p. 51)

Sports Training Tip

A coach must always be a student. Sports training knowledge is always changing. A coach must move with the times and embrace the sports science and technology that exists.

Reflecting on the Needs of the Athlete

As indicated, coaching style has to mesh with the biological maturity, training maturity, psychology, life stage and personality of the athlete/team members being coached (the so-called 'developmental' factors). Among these developmental factors are numerous stressors that can affect the athlete (and coach). These must be considered. It will often be easier to do this with older athletes, who can express themselves (should they wish). Issues such as moving house, getting a new job, relationship problems and exams can all be verbalised to the coach, who can adapt training accordingly. It is important at times like this that coach and athlete agree on realistic expectations. The problems start to arise when the athlete does not (or will not) communicate with the coach, or if unrealistic expectations, sports-wise, are established.

Adolescents bring with them potentially different and perhaps more difficult sets of experiences for the coach to deal with. They will be experiencing considerable life-changing and personality-defining events, and will be literally changing before the eyes of the coach. In circumstances such as these, successful coaching may involve counselling and talking to parents, perhaps even adopting a more laissez-faire approach for a while (as long as the athlete's safety is maintained). The idea is to 'get the athlete through' a particular transition while not losing them to sport.

Dealing with Family and Friends

Parents/guardians and others close to the young athlete naturally want the best for them, but some may take this a little too far and become overly pushy. In doing so they may interfere with the coaching process. A parent may decide, for example, that more training is needed for their child, and this may lead to poor performance, injury or burnout. The key to minimising this and other similar scenarios is to involve and inform parents as to what you, as coach, are trying to achieve.

Parents could be made to feel more involved by taking part in the session. This works especially well in large groups. However, the coach must trust the parents, and the parents must do what the coach has asked of them (it may be necessary to check insurances in certain instances, to be on the safe side – if problems are encountered the parent could be encouraged to take a relevant coaching qualification).

Adopting a Teamwork Approach to Coaching

Coaches, whatever their sport, should not be fearful of obtaining advice/help from other coaches/experts. No coach 'knows everything'. They may not be great on nutrition, for example, so referring the athlete to a nutritionist would make a great deal of sense. Making the services of a sports massage expert available provides another avenue of support. A coach should strive to maximise the performance of those they coach. They should not be blinkered by ego, and potentially hold back an athlete because they do not want to get help from elsewhere.

Sports Training Tip

The coach should always be wary of providing too much feedback as this may confuse, rather than ease, the athlete's understanding. Rather, the coach should try to focus the athlete on a key aspect of, for example, technique. If the focus of a high jump session is on plant, take-off and knee drive, then changing focus to bar clearance and layout is best avoided (unless after a few jumps the former aspects are being perfectly performed!). Very few athletes (including those at elite level) will be able to hold on to all the feedback a coach may want to give them.

The Athlete's Long-term Development

Although parents (and coaches) may like to produce, for example, an under-16 national track champion, they would probably not be so keen to do so if they realised that this could jeopardise the potential of the athlete to win an Olympic medal 10 years later. The athlete needs to be nurtured and taken through transitory phases in order to maximise their potential when it really matters.

Child Protection

In this day and age, coaches are usually subjected to police checks by sports governing bodies. Children obviously need to be protected and parents reassured that all will be safe. However, coaches can be put in very difficult situations when it comes to voluntary disclosures on the part of young athletes. If, for example, an under-18 year-old starts to discuss something that involves abuse allegations or other highly personal issues, I recommend that they are stopped before they are able to tell the whole story. The coach should inform them that if they continue, they may have no other option but to go to the relevant authorities. Child protection means just that – a disclosure cannot be shelved. It may jeopardise the coach/athlete relationship at the time but this is better than jeopardising the coach's reputation/permission to coach or the health/security of the child.

Sports Training Tip

Coaches should develop their questioning skills. They should avoid the use of too many closed or leading questions, such as, 'Your foot position was good when you hit that forehand volley, what do you think?' Rather, questions that encourage the athlete to reflect and focus (open questions) are much more likely to elicit a positive, useable response. A much better question would be, 'How did you feel about that forehand volley, in terms of ball contact?' After the athlete has responded, the coach could then follow up, as they felt necessary, by prompting, for example, 'and what about your foot position?'

Recording Coaching Information

Coaches should maintain an electronic or written log of their training plans and sessions. This will provide them with a valuable bank of knowledge, which they will continually be able to refer to and apply. If time allows, the coach should fill out an evaluation sheet for each workout. Depending on the age of the athlete, the coach may also get them to do similar (athletes, particularly in individual and quantitative sports such as rowing, should be completing their own training diaries). I have provided a sample workout evaluation sheet below. It can of course be varied in regard to specific sports.

Coach Training Workout Evaluation Sheet

Date and time:

Venue:

Weather conditions:

Athletes:

Session

Session goal/goals:

Session evaluation

Part 1: Record the actuality of the workout (e.g. times achieved, weight lifted)

Part 2: Evaluate how you felt the session went in regard to the pre-established goals

---

Your own evaluation

Using the following evaluation scale, rate how you coached the session against the coaching aspects managing, teaching, communicating:

Evaluation scale

1	2	3	4	5
not satisfactory	satisfactory	more than satisfactory	very satisfactory	excellent

Managing

Communicating

Teaching

Record any comments/explanations

_____

Identify any area you need as coach to follow up (whether this be for yourself or for the athlete/athletes):

English Institute of Sport http://www.eis2win. co.uk/ The English Institute of Sport notes that it is at the forefront of the quiet revolution that will change the face of sport in this country.' It is a nationwide network of world-class support services, designed to foster the talent of elite athletes. The site has useful information for coaches and athletes.

British Coaching Sports Coach UK (formerly National Coaching Foundation) http://www. sportscoachuk.org Sports Coach UK was established to provide non-sport-specific information at a number of levels to cater for all coaches, from the beginner to the top level national coach. They run numerous courses that will help develop generic coaching skills. Courses include: 'Good Practice and Child Protection', 'How to Coach Disabled People in Sport'.

Sport England http://www.sportengland.org Sport England is an organisation committed to creating opportunities for people to start in sport, stay in sport and succeed in sport. Sport England promotes and invests in sport and is responsible for delivering the government's sporting objectives.

Peak Performance http://www.pponline.co.uk A sport science website for athletes, trainers and coaches of all disciplines, devoted to improving stamina, strength and fitness and the treatment of injuries. Peak Performance also publishes monthly newsletters packed with useful information for coaches, and is responsible for numerous ancillary websites, all related to coaching, sport and fitness.

National Strength and Conditioning Association (USA) http://www.nsca-lift.org Leading authority on strength and conditioning. Provides information to its members and the public.

Speed, Agility and Quickness Training http:// www.saqinternational.com Runs courses aimed at improving 'SAQ' for various sports.

Sports Websites with Information on Specific Coaching

Athletics http://www.ukathletics.net
Basketball http://www.englandbasketball.co.uk
Football http://www.thefa.com
Rowing http://www.ara-rowing.org
Rugby Union http://www.rfu.com
Squash http://www.englandsquash.com
Tennis http://www.lta.org.uk

INDEX

NOTES

NOTES

NOTES

NOTES